VALUES WE HOLD DEAR

Inspiring Stories to Reconnect America

KYLE A. STONE

"Values We Hold Dear" is a book with an incomparable, unique focus on values and timeless virtues. Kyle A. Stone gives rise to the need of our great Nation. He makes us mindful that our Nation is founded on "Life, Liberty and the pursuit of Happiness" but that it is now threatened by becoming off course.

Kyle's narration will bless you with inspirational true short stories that can inspire and can help us work towards restoration of our beautiful country. His book is a call to us to return to values rooted in truth, wisdom, moderation, justice and courage once again—first personally—then collectively as, "We The People." These values were first put into place by our Founding Fathers and they are the very divine virtues that they sacrificed for. The virtues given our Nation are God inspired and God blessed. They were woven into the fabric of the American and of who we are. For us to fully appreciate the blessings of liberty now, requires our help. We can accomplish that through our unique and personal healing and mindset. We can learn while studying the stories just how we can acquire greater strength, awareness and fortitude. Then, through action of returning to our timeless values and virtues, we can restore what our men in war fought to maintain for us. There is much that we all can do to help heal our nation and our world. Our work can begin in our own communities. Reading this elegantly crafted and insightful book, we will learn of ideas that can help us restore our Nation—our world. May we not remain on a path of destruction. Let us do our part. "Ripple on."

Betty J Eadie
International Best Selling Author
"Embraced by the Light"

Values We Hold Dear © Copyright 2023 VWHD Enterprises LLC

For more information, email valuesweholddear@protonmail.com.

ISBN: 979-8-88759-733-1 - paperback

ISBN: 979-8-88759-734-8 - ebook

Library of Congress Control Number: 2023907910

Get Your Free Gift!

To get the best experience with this book, I've found readers who download, print, and use these guiding values and workbook, are able to implement and take the necessary steps needed to revive the American nation.

In This House We...

- Believe in GOD, Faith, Miracles, Prayer & Objective Science
- Support the U.S. Constitution & Learn Accurate U.S. History
- Honor the U.S. Declaration of Independence & Founding Fathers
- Stand for Old Glory
- Believe in Education & Critical Thinking, Not Indoctrination
- Support Local Businesses & Capitalism to Build Community
- Support the Military, Local Law Enforcement & First Responders
- Recognize Every Life Has Value & Reject Racism
- Embrace Responsibility, Reject Victimhood
- Believe Men & Women Are Equal
- Believe in Charity, Love, Respect, Kindness & Living Aloha

VERITAS ★ HONOR ★ DEFENSORE
www.ValuesWeHoldDear.com

You can get a copy by visiting:
www.ValuesWeHoldDear.com

Dedication

To my Heavenly Father for the inspiration and miracles in bringing this work about in a most challenging year.

To the Founding Fathers, their wives, and courageous Americans throughout history who, through virtue, forged a great nation.

To my wife, Jamie, for her love and support.

Acknowledgments

Thank you to Ralph Cochran for encouraging me to think bigger.

Thank you to my Turley Talks Mastermind friends and friends and family who consistently encouraged and provided meaningful feedback.

Thank you to my aides, Rodney Steward, PhD, Camille Von Nieda, Emily Shai, and Deanna Weigel for their great ideas, feedback and efforts to making this work come alive.

Thank you to Betty Eadie and Jeffrey Thomason for their insightful reviews and suggestions.

A deep thank you to Steve Turley, PhD for the abbreviated, but vital classical education training and current event framing to help me "connect the dots" to produce this work.

"With public Spirit let each Bosom glow
And Love of Liberty direct the blow Rouse,
patriot Heroes and pursue the plan
Teach listless Souls what 'tis to play the man!"
(1776 American Revolutionary War Era Poem)

Pieatas
Latin root of Patriotism—Love of and Duty to God,
Neighbor, and Country.

"It does not take a majority to prevail ... but rather an irate,
tireless minority, keen on setting brushfires of freedom
in the minds of men."
–Samuel Adams

Bondage is easy. Freedom takes passionate effort!
–Author

Table of Contents

Foreword

The Air of Freedom

"Truth will ultimately prevail
where there is pains to bring it to light."
General George Washington

One of my favorite books is J.R.R. Tolkien's *The Two Towers*, the second of the three-book epic *The Lord of the Rings*. And one of my favorite scenes in the story is Gandalf's visit to King Théoden at his court in Edoras, the capital of the Kingdom of Rohan. Entering the Golden Hall of Meduseld, Gandalf and his entourage encounter a king that had long been suffering from a spell-induced senility cast upon him by the dark forces of the evil Saruman and his servant Wormtongue. With the king sidelined by demonic dementia, these dark forces were unleashed to take over the kingdom.

However, unbeknownst to Wormtongue, Gandalf hid his magical staff under his cloak, successfully smuggling it into the king's court:

He raised his staff. Thunder rolled. The sunlight was blotted out from the eastern windows; the whole hall became suddenly dark as night. The fire faded to sullen embers. Only Gandalf could be seen, standing white and tall before the blackened hearth. 'Now Théoden son of Thengel, will you hearken to me?' said Gandalf … 'I bid you come out before your doors and look abroad. Too long have you sat in shadows and trusted to twisted tales and crooked promptings.'

Slowly Théoden left his chair. A faint light grew in the hall again. His beloved niece hastened to the king's side, taking his arm, and with faltering steps the old man came down from the dais and paced softly through the hall. Wormtongue remained lying on the floor. They came to the doors and Gandalf knocked. 'Open!' he cried. 'The Lord of the Mark comes forth!' The doors rolled back and a keen air came whistling in. A wind was blowing on the hill.

'Now, lord,' said Gandalf, 'look out upon your land! Breathe the free air again!'

'It is not so dark here,' said Théoden.

'No,' said Gandalf. 'Nor does age lie so heavily on your shoulders as some would have you think. Cast aside your prop!'

From the king's hand the black staff fell clattering on the stones. He drew himself up, slowly, as a man that is stiff from long bending over some dull toil. Now tall and straight he stood, and his eyes were blue as he looked into the opening sky.

'Dark have been my dreams of late,' he said, 'but I feel as one new-awakened.'

The power of this scene is in the way Tolkien recognizes the profound connection between memory and civilization. Having effectively darkened the king's remembrance, malevolent forces were able to manipulate him in accordance with their sinister schemes and effectively take over his sovereign realm. The loss of King Théoden's memory entailed the very loss of his identity and, in turn, the loss of the character of his kingdom.

This connection between memory and civilization was hardly lost on our Founding Fathers. They were profoundly grateful caretakers of the rich moral, philosophical, and political inheritance of Western civilization, a civilization centered on the three ancient worlds of Jerusalem, Athens, and Rome. Cultural memory, particularly rooted in the great virtue traditions, was considered essential to maintaining and perpetuating a political freedom indicative of the heirs of such cities.

However, over the last several decades, the dark clouds of a radical secularization have eclipsed this civilizational vision, a secularization rooted in the cultural Marxist ideology of Hungarian writer György Lukács and the Italian philosopher Antonio Gramsci. Their radical ideas were brought to the

United States during WWII by members of what's called the Frankfurt School, a think tank at Goethe University

Frankfurt comprised of some of the top Marxist thinkers such as Max Horkheimer, Theodor Adorno, Wilhelm Reich, Herbert Marcuse, and Erich Fromm. What made these Marxists unique is that they all believed that *culture* rather than *class* was the primary location for the historical battle between the bourgeoisie and the proletariat.

They came to American university campuses and developed and refined the notion of what they called "critical theory." The guiding principle of critical theory was the assumption that America was inherently oppressive, that its laws, its institutions, its founding documents, and its leaders are all products of and manifest that oppression. György Lukács was hardly shy in revealing the entire purpose of this theory as articulated in his work "Mon chemin vers Mark": "I saw the revolutionary destruction of society as the one and only solution to the cultural contradictions of the epoch" and "Such a worldwide overturning of values cannot take place without the annihilation of the old values and the creation of new ones by the revolutionaries."[1]

Critical theory has since infected virtually every aspect of university education and has most recently manifested itself in K-12 public school classrooms in the form of critical race theory and radical transgender activism. Through such

---

1 György Lukacs, "Mon chemin vers Marx" (1969), Nouvelles Etudes hongroises (Budapest, 1973), 8:78–79, cited in Michael Löwy, Georg Lukács—From Romanticism to Bolshevism, trans. Patrick Camiller (London: NLB, 1979), 93.

a radicalized educational system, the whole of professional life—politics, media, business, law, entertainment—has had the memory of what it means to be American wiped away, succumbing to a thoroughly anti-western, anti-American, and anti-Christian woke Marxism rooted in victimhood, resentment, and, ultimately, cancel culture. For as Lukács made clear, the entire goal of cultural Marxism is to destroy and annihilate the very foundations of our culture, which means that the ultimate goal of cancel culture *is the canceling of Western civilization itself.*

And yet, to the shock of liberal politicians and pundits alike, that very civilization they thought they had buried has begun to reawaken. Scholars have increasingly recognized a social and cultural trend known as "retraditionalization," which involves more and more populations rejecting the woke secularism of radical leftists and returning instead to nation, culture, custom, and tradition. As such, the old religions that founded the great world civilizations are reviving, along with a comparable resuscitation of those very civilizations as well.

This book by Kyle A. Stone is a gem within this reawakening. In many respects, *The Values We Hold Dear* is much akin to a visit by Gandalf to a delirious citizenry. By opening this book, one encounters a treasure trove of historical narratives and events that weave together a cultural memory that can well serve to awaken us from our secular stupor and reacquaint us with our true American identity.

Kyle's masterful retelling of the stories of these ordinary men and women who did such extraordinary things is a collective call, a summons that, if heeded, will most certainly dispel the darkness of our age, and reminds us all of who we really are and the glorious inheritance to which we belong. It is my hope that with the turning of each page, you will be all the more inspired to rise up, abandon the secular shadows, confidently walk into the light of day, and breathe the air of freedom once again.

Dr. Steve Turley

We Have Been Here Before (Introduction)

Let virtue guide your thoughts. Let sacrifice and love motivate citizenship. Let faith nourish freedom.

*T*HESE are the times that try men's souls. The summer soldier and the sunshine patriot will, in this crisis, shrink from the service of their country; but he that stands by it now, deserves the love and thanks of man and woman. Tyranny, like hell, is not easily conquered; yet we have this consolation with us, that the harder the conflict, the more glorious the triumph. What we obtain too cheap, we esteem too lightly: it is <u>dearness</u> only that gives everything its <u>value</u>. Heaven knows how to put a proper price upon its goods; and it would be strange indeed if so celestial an article as FREEDOM should not be highly rated" (Paine 2012, 180).

These eloquent words, written in 1776 in Pennsylvania as General Washington's army camped in winter quarters, hauntingly reverberate in the halls of our history and echo to us even in this present moment.

Indeed, 1775–1776 were difficult years for the glorious struggle for liberty.

The repressive colonial government took great measures to keep the colony of Massachusetts under its thumb. The professional but cruel Army of British Redcoats and the Colonial Farmers exchanged the first rounds of the long-simmering War in Lexington. King George III and Parliament committed to quell the American rebellion by sending the largest contingent of tens of thousands of British sailors, Marines, and Army the world had ever seen, transporting this impressive force across the Atlantic to demonstrate, in no uncertain terms, their resolve.

And demonstrate the British did. British forces faced the colonial militia at Breed's Hill and Bunker Hill, winning a costly and bloody battle outside the city of Boston. Later, thousands of British troops landed in New York City. The masts of hundreds of transport ships arrived in New York City in late summer, dotting the harbor and giving the massive fleet the appearance of a leafless, water-drowned studded forest.

The British Officer General Howe drove General George Washington's fledgling Continental army from New York. Only by the hand of Providence did Washington's Army escape the jaws of permanent defeat.

And here, in the frigid, wintery Pennsylvania colony, laid the ragtag army freezing, bloody, some shoeless, frostbitten, hunkering down in bitter winter conditions in a baren woodland by a river. General Washington publicly did his very best to keep morale up for the troops but privately confided in a personal letter to his brother that the "game was about up" (Washington 1776). Knowing enlistments were set to expire less than a week away—which would significantly reduce his troop strength—General Washington, with trepidation, decided to gamble it all. A plan that might make a difference or end in ruination, forever damning the Glorious Cause. It was a desperate measure; however, as is so often the case in war, desperate measures are sometimes necessary. And so it was that on that fateful Christmas night, under the cover of darkness and a shroud of secrecy, General Washington led his troops across the river and into legend.

A dangerous plan, indeed. In secret, Washington confided in a small group of trusted officers. The best troops would cross an icy river during a Nor'easter wintery Christmas night to fight the feared and despised but professionally competent German Hessian mercenaries hired by the Crown along with their dreaded yet exceptional commanding officer Col. Johann Rall. General Washington gambled on one last hope.

Miraculously, the gambit succeeded. The daring crossing of the Delaware River stunned the Hessian troops. The Continentals killed Col. Rall in action. This one effort breathed new life into the cause of liberty. Reenlistments surged, and new enlistments increased the size of the army. The French, the colonies' eventual ally, took notice. A renewed spirit awakened from the victorious efforts in Trenton, New Jersey. Momentum built for victory begets victory.

Fellow citizens and patriots, it is no exaggeration to say that we are fighting for the very soul of our republic. The Founding Fathers crafted a system of government designed to protect the rights of the people and prevent the abuse of power. But today, we face the very real danger of losing those protections.

At every turn, tyranny, lies, spin, injustice, and abuse of government power are present in every corner. The powerful corporate and political elite have established a two-tiered justice system: one for themselves, where their gross and obvious crimes are swept under the rug, and another system of justice for the rest of us.

As examples, if the average citizen trades stocks with secret or non-public knowledge about the organization, that's called "insider trading" and the person could be fined or jailed. But, if a member of the permanent political class executes stock trades based on specialized knowledge they acquire while holding office, they become very wealthy, with no repercussions. If the average professional that holds a coveted, government authorized security clearance accidently mishandles classified information, they are fined, fired and can be jailed with their career prospects in tatters. However, if a member of the professional political class intentionally mishandles classified information, and even tries to hide that they mishandled the information, they are given a mild rebuke or excused without legal consequences.

But worse, if the average citizen speaks of these egregious violations by the political class, the media mob and their vicious mouth-pieces label the content "misinformation", and promote "fact checking" by unknown and unaccountable so called "experts." The end result being the person becomes ostracized (aka cancelled) and demeaned. The demonization of average citizens and the weaponization of the law in order to suppress and force compliance abounds. Sadly, the willful suppression of freedom of speech by agencies and governmental bodies using the quaint but deceptive term "misinformation" is now common. And tragically, outright lies and twisted truths about the founding of the United States of America proliferate and are wrongly celebrated in our media and classrooms. It seems that defeat is inevitable.

But my countrymen, we have been here before. We, have been here, before.

Where o where are the men and women of the American Republic? Where o where are the sons and daughters of liberty? Where o where are the winter patriots who will stand by the Values, We Hold Dear?

Arise, awaken, learn, build, and lead! Your day is here! All is not lost unless *you allow it to be so.* It is up to you now. Like Paul Revere's and William Dawes's horse-galloping ride through the Massachusetts countryside, we should be shouting, "The enemy is here!" We should be gathering. Be not a sunshine patriot.

We bow to no man! We do NOT submit to a globalist system or enterprise! We hold these truths to be self-evident.

We are endowed by our Creator—not politicians, not individuals, not wealthy organizations—with Life, Liberty, and the pursuit of Happiness! Further, and importantly, we are obligated to generations before us and to our posterity and future generations to defend these rights and our freedom of Conscience! You are *liber*; you are free!

We, have been here before. *Alas, what can you do?*

The following true stories from the history of the United States of America are set forth for you to inspire and educate with calls to action. They are a spark of passion for learning, connecting history to the present, inspiring deeds, and are designed to ignite the patriotic fires within your souls—the same fires that burned within Samuel Adams, Patrick Henry, and Thomas Jefferson.

Within this work are virtuous truths. These are truths you *instinctively* recognize because they are eternal and thus internal. These truths maximize personal and community happiness through free agency, not by force. Many of you realize, see, or even feel the path the United States is on leads the nation to a destructive tailspin economically, morally, and even defensively. Philosophies and alternative values wholly detached from virtue, truth, and reality pollute our society and culture. We are buried today in a culture of cynicism, propaganda, and literal and purposeful destruction, where communities, law and order, and human life are commodities to be used, abused, and rejected or "canceled" when no longer deemed of value. We have seen this play out anciently in Rome and Greece. We have seen this play out within the last 100 years in Stalin's Russia, Hitler's Germany, Mao's China, Minh's Vietnam, and Castro's Cuba, where millions upon millions were killed or starved in service to tyrannical views of the "greater good." This is not only disastrous for the United States and our families, but it also has dangerous ramifications for liberty-loving peoples globally.

These true stories from America's past connect ancient wisdom and the heart of virtuous learning to the Founding Fathers and from the Founding Fathers to you, the present-day citizen. The Founders warned us of the time in which we now live. We have disconnected from these values and virtuous truths. To survive, we must repair the chains and reconnect to the anchors, or our security and happiness will disappear. Like the minutemen of old, we are called to action to re-anchor our society to our treasured roots. For the young reader, your strength and courage are needed to change course.

Another way to view this work, these stories are medicine. They are an inscribed balm, an antidote to counter the venomous poison injected into the culture by the perpetually aggrieved, the destroyers of traditions, and the unwise and devious officials that peddle in real "misinformation" to further their political aims to increase their pocketbook. The stories are prescriptions to counter the propaganda. Further, they counter nation-states and global organizations—private and public, American and foreign—that lie to you. For they want you suppressed, silenced, and reduced to serfdom, to merely become a number without identity—producers and consumers designed to labor for their personal enrichment.

This medicine is designed to be proliferated and shared with millions of your fellow American citizens. Readers of this work who are not American, such as our brothers and sisters in Canada, New Zealand, and Australia, or *any* person who loves the blessing of true freedom, this work is for you as well. For while the Founders designed the U.S. Constitution and Declaration of Independence for America, its principles and precepts apply to all men and women equally, for they are eternal. Finally, this work is made to inspire a younger generation to shake off the chains of apathy that weigh them down, to encourage them to engage in meaningful relationships, to be healthy—mentally and physically—and to serve a cause much larger than themselves.

These stories will stimulate awareness of the precarious situation we are in and help you appreciate that true citizenship has a price—that liberty and freedom are never free and constant vigilance is required to protect them. These stories will give you perspective, wisdom, and, most importantly, hope and courage with a spur to action. Anciently wisdom, moderation, justice, and courage were considered the pillars of virtue, courage being the most vital (Philo, Scaura, and Brutus 2019). The Founding Fathers subscribed to the Greek philosopher Aristotle's view of virtue, that true happiness is achieved when "the activity of the soul is in perfect harmony with virtue." This work is a contribution to the body of thought and work to perpetuate courage. Courage is the most important virtue on which all others survive to promote and defend true individual liberty, the right to the freedom of speech, and a strong community and nation grounded in ancient and divine virtues.

We live in perilous times, and you are needed to stand firm and push back. This work will help you do so. Consider how far we, as a nation, have fallen. Socrates powerfully illustrates how nations fall in the ancient work, THE REPUBLIC. First, the "aristocratic" constitution, meaning the constitution produced by wise leaders—like our founders— degenerates into the timocratic or "honor-loving" when the military class "prevails over" the wise. Wisdom, humility, temperance, and reason are lost as they are replaced by love of glory and ambition.

Second, the timocratic constitution "degenerates" into oligarchy, the rule of the wealthy few. The middle class is dismantled, and the poor become the masses. Oligarchs rule the poor masses with an eye and heart fixated on money. Greed, hubris, haughtiness, and avarice abound in oligarchies. Oligarchs scheme, "How can I make more money and gain more power," without thought to morals or consequences of their actions.

Third, the poor masses eventually revolt against the oligarchs in abject anger. The oligarch constitution degenerates into democracy, the rule of the people. The people, enflamed with passion and lacking wisdom and reason (as the rule of the wise has now been long forgotten), govern its democratic constitution in whatever way the winds blow—to their demise.

Forth, eventually, the democratic constitution degenerates as the masses follow orators with cunning, beautiful rhetoric, thus planting the seed of tyranny. They convince the uneasy, ungrounded masses, for the people have lost understanding of their culture, customs, and traditions. For when the democratic constitution fails, *as it always does, it is replaced with tyranny* (Plato 1959).

But take courage! What is the prize for your efforts as you learn, build, lead, and take personal action? A glorious resurrection of our Declaration of Independence, our Constitution, the vindication of the Founding Founders, our right of Conscience, our rights to free agency, the securing of blessings for our posterity, and, as Thomas Paine rightly put it, the FREEDOM to practice, promote, and preach the Values We Hold Dear. Once again, free and fair elections will uphold accountable leaders who understand and live the timeless, virtuous principles of wisdom, temperance, justice, and courage. The population will also live these virtues. Truth will be free and will be spoken again in love and power. No more will today's standing army of agents be independent of and superior to the civil power. The people will no longer be serfs in their own land.

As Mr. Todd Beamer stated while flying aboard the highjacked jet plane, United 93, over a Pennsylvania field on September 11, 2001, "Let's roll." Todd and his fellow passengers' selfless actions and sacrifice saved lives; will yours?

Figure 1. General Washington Crossing the Delaware River Christmas Day 1776

(Purchased Alamy.com 23 Sept. 2022)

The Crossing

Believe in GOD, Faith, Miracles, Prayer, &
Objective Science

(Be Grateful & Humble in Trials)

*M*ajor life changes or traumas can be excruciating, but hard personal trials prepare us for something much greater. For in these trials, we learn truths. We learn about ourselves and how much strength lies within us. If we allow it, we learn of the goodness of something much larger than ourselves, our Creator, the interconnectedness as humans on this sojourn of life, the importance of kindness, truth, beauty, love, and service to others.

Further, *as we bear it well*, we can be *grateful*. Indeed, we learn to be grateful, like this little band of 17th-century wayfarers.

✳✳✳

Their lives were miserable. Their journey, unbearable. The frigid nights, the rolling high seas emanating a chilling spindrift of cold mist onto the ship's deck from the lifeless gray North Atlantic, the cussing from the ship's crew, and the near starvation combined created a pitiful sight. Worse, though, was the thought of what awaited ... the desolate wilderness. Nonetheless, this disheveled group of passengers was well prepared for a life of struggle and hardships.

Only 14 years prior, the persecuted ragtag group of 102 experienced something similar. Leaving their homes after intense persecutions in the farming community of Scrooby, Nottinghamshire, England, they survived vile threats from cruel countrymen and severe persecution from agents of the Crown. They lost nearly everything due to a thieving seafaring captain, who turned them in to authorities and stole all of their property. They endured jail for their faith and suffered unjustified and unspeakable abuse.

Finally, they left their homeland on two ships to a new country. Enroute, this tousled band experienced hunger and thirst. They endured the despising glares and haughtiness of the ship's crew, who laughed, mocked, and used vile language to these religious souls to insult them as seasickness involuntarily gripped their weak frames with all manner of illness and vileness. The group narrowly escaped the Grim Reaper's scythe by surviving the wrath of a powerful sea storm that nearly wrecked the smelly, small, cramped 17th-century sailing vessels. Yet, they persevered, making it to their destination poor, starved, and cold. They arrived in a strange but beautiful European city with the elegant 12th-century gothic church spires and neatly lined homes to greet them. Leiden, Holland, had a different tongue and customs, but the group thought this might be their new home where they could practice their faith in peace.

However, not long after their arrival did it become clear; the locals held them with contempt as the city swelled with new inhabitants and refugees. Further, their labors to earn a basic living were grueling. In Leiden, their wages could not sustain them. To add to their woes, these pioneers were deeply concerned about the unsavory influences the city had on their children. So, many moved inland to the Netherlands countryside.

Alas, while more affordable and easier to acquire property, the challenges remained. A strange land, a strange tongue, and now their children started to openly reject the "old ways" of their community's values, faith, and beliefs. However, what options did this community have?

Rumors spread about a new land! The King of England chartered a company to establish a commercial colony in the new region. A few in the community opined that perhaps moving to this untamed wilderness might be best for them. A new opportunity, a new start! But many in this group vigorously opposed it. How would they survive in this new land? There would be no inns to greet them, no roads to trod on, no established farms to be fed, and no homes with hearths to keep them warm during cold nights. "No! We are too poor; we cannot move." The community decided to stay in Holland.

Yet, important events transpired beyond their control. The Dutch people no longer wanted them in Holland.

Further, Holland neared war with the powerful kingdom of Spain. The corrupting influence of the Dutch culture on their children persisted, with older children leaving their parents and the community, forever rejecting the values with which they were raised. The little community became convinced— to survive and to be able to practice their faith and protect their customs and traditions, they must once again remove themselves from their modest but fairly comfortable lives and leave for the unknown.

This beleaguered group boarded two small sailing vessels near where they had arrived only 12 years earlier. But they did not get very far. One of the vessels immediately began to leak uncontrollably. Not an ideal start on a voyage due to take months across an ocean. Turning back, the vessel's captain ordered repairs. After the repairs, they set out again. Alas, the same issue on the same vessel—a substantial leak! And again, they turned back for repairs—bad omen with fall rapidly approaching. Regrettably, the vessel had a construction flaw and deemed unsuitable for the long voyage. This meant some in this small community would have to be left behind.

The healthier, skilled, and more fit members set sail in the early fall of 1620. Knowing from experience the travails of seafaring travel but determined to live a life of faith, holding fast to their belief in their Creator's providential hands, they crossed from the old world to the new (Bradford 1898).

"Land Ho!" came the welcomed cry from the sailing vessel crows nest atop the main mast. A miracle! Pleadings with the Lord had been answered. Rushing to the front of the boat, a young maiden named Mary Chilton, an important figure and fore-mother of American history, determined she would be one of the first pilgrims to touch her feet on the land, and as soon as the opportunity arose, leapt ashore (Adams 1884, 380). After the wretched ordeal, all the sea-wary passengers found their way ashore after long, grueling months on a cold December day. They calmly and humbly knelt and offered a prayer of gratitude to God for their safe arrival. Despite the Mayflower being off course for the planned destination of Jamestown, Virginia, the Pilgrims offered thanks in what is now known as Cape Cod, Massachusetts (Bradford 1898).

Patriots, a time for reflection and action.

Faith and gratitude are formidable weapons as well as salves to the wounded. Faith provides a light of hope to grieving souls. Sometimes it is hard to see it or understand how to reach that light, but faith gives you motivation and drive to keep moving forward. Gratitude reminds you of what is important and what you are fighting for. Further, gratitude heals trauma and helps you move beyond loss or sorrow.

Reflect for a moment on hard challenges you have experienced. As tough as these challenges were or perhaps even are, think about how these hard things wisen us, humble us, temper us, and give us perspective. If we allow, the challenges make us stronger and more courageous to face even the hardest trials life throws at us. This includes the trials we face as a nation today. Starting the day with a spirit of gratitude helps set your day, and gives you perspective on the good in your life.

Consider the privations of the Pilgrims 15 years and the arduous Mayflower sailing. The previous adversities immensely prepared these pilgrims for the extreme hardships. Grateful for this difficult 15-year journey; this hearty band thanked God for the miracle of the landing. They practiced gratitude every day, despite the constant hardships and abuse.

Gratitude is instinctual, natural, and even reflexive. Former U.S. Ambassador to Slovenia, Joseph Mussomeli (2020), wrote, "Gratitude remains the only key that unshackles us and lets us breathe free …We all unthinkingly use the phrase 'the gift of life,' but it is only a gift if we really think of it as such. If we don't, then life is an unbearable curse … No matter how bountiful and varied our good fortune, life has no flavor and is devoid of any joy unless we are grateful for it." Being grateful is a vital and healing virtue. Medical professionals and psychologists have long observed how the happier and healthier in our society practice daily gratitude ("Giving Thanks" 2021). Suffering souls are able to bear their trials and hardships with dignity, with an eye toward hope with gratitude. Like the Pilgrims before us, are not the American people in need of healing? As a nation, have we not become intemperate and haughty, and have we lost this reflective attitude that the Pilgrims so freely expressed?

We know from the writings of Governor William Bradford that the Pilgrims suffered much more in the years to come, including starvation, a frigid winter, and disease, which nearly wiped them out. Finally, they found a respite from suffering in November 1623 and feasted for three days with a native New England tribe, to what in our tradition is the First Thanksgiving.

It bears reminding for accuracy that the First Thanksgiving was about the Pilgrims thanking their Creator and God for surviving their years of *trials*, keeping true to their *faith,* and the much-needed bountiful harvest. The First Thanksgiving was not, as *critics wrongly and inaccurately attribute to the Pilgrims*, a celebration of the slaughter of Pequot natives in Groton, Connecticut, during a time of great tension between the native inhabitants and the English settlers. Indeed, this is a gross falsehood taught by too many in our educational institutions and proliferates in today's social media (Gosling 2018).

As you read the following Proclamation below, ponder and share with your loved ones what you are thankful for in wonder and humility. Do this daily. Young men and women, teenagers, practice this principle early and often and see how it enriches your lives. Adults, teach this to your children and grandchildren.

Healing of the nation starts here. One can choose to live a life in perpetual anger, complaining with deep vitriol that life is unfair. This is how the ever-aggrieved gain power over the poor. This anger only leads to misery and despair and a sense of entitlement. Further, it leads to physical and mental illness as well as hate. Is it not better, regardless of your personal faith, to start from a place of awe and wonder like the ancients encouraged?

What are you willing to do and continue to do to show gratitude for the blessings you have and the trials that have made you better, stronger, and wiser? Are you willing to practice giving thanks daily to make your lives and the lives of your families and countrymen better? Doing so will strengthen your community, which is foundational to healing the nation.

Make gratitude a habit.

"[President] Washington issued a proclamation on October 3, 1789, designating Thursday, November 26, as a national day of thanks. In his proclamation, Washington declared that the necessity for such a day sprung from the Almighty's care of Americans prior to the Revolution, assistance to them in achieving independence, and help in establishing the constitutional government."

By the President of the United States of America, a Proclamation.

Whereas it is the duty of all Nations to acknowledge the providence of Almighty God, to obey his will, to be grateful for his benefits, and humbly to implore his protection and favor—and whereas both Houses of Congress have by their joint Committee requested me to recommend to the People of the United States a day of public thanksgiving and prayer to be observed by acknowledging with grateful hearts the many signal favors of Almighty God especially by affording them an opportunity peaceably to establish a form of government for their safety and happiness.

Now therefore I do recommend and assign Thursday the 26th day of November next to be devoted by the People of these States to the service of that great and glorious Being, who is the beneficent Author of all the good that was, that is, or that will be—That we may then all unite in rendering unto him our sincere and humble thanks—for his kind care and protection of the People of this Country previous to their becoming a Nation— for the signal and manifold mercies, and the favorable interpositions of his Providence which we experienced in the course and conclusion of the late war—for the great degree of tranquility, union, and plenty, which we have since enjoyed—for the peaceable and rational manner, in which we have been enabled to establish constitutions of government for our safety and happiness, and particularly the national One now lately instituted—for the civil and religious liberty with which we are blessed; and the means we have of acquiring and diffusing useful knowledge; and in general for all the great and various favors which he hath been pleased to confer upon us.

And also that we may then unite in most humbly offering our prayers and supplications to the great Lord and Ruler of Nations and beseech him to pardon our national and other transgressions—to enable us all, whether in public or private stations, to perform our several and relative duties properly and punctually—to render our national government a blessing to all the people, by constantly being a Government of wise, just, and constitutional laws, discreetly and faithfully executed and obeyed—to protect and guide all Sovereigns and Nations (especially such as have shewn kindness unto us) and to bless them with good government, peace, and concord—To promote the knowledge and practice of true religion and virtue, and the increase of science among them and us—and generally to grant unto all Mankind such a degree of temporal prosperity as he alone knows to be best.

Given under my hand at the City of New York the third day of October in the year of our Lord 1789.

Go: Washington

("Thanksgiving Proclamation" 2022)

Figure 2. The Pilgrims in Holland circa 1607 (Purchased Alamy.com 23 Sept. 2022)

Figure 3. Mary Chilton and Pilgrims landing at Cape Code, MA 1621 (Purchased Alamy.com 23 Sept. 2022)

Mary White Rowlandson

Believe in GOD, Faith, Miracles,
Prayer & Objective Science

(Expect Miracles)

aving faith or belief in miracles may seem quaint, silly, or even crazy in today's world. Many mock the supernatural or belief in a higher power, disdainfully claiming miracles do not happen. However, isn't it amazing when ordinary people of little or no faith suddenly become awakened or even shaken to the spiritual core and alter their lives for the better, particularly after trauma or tragedy? Even the survival of the Mayflower Pilgrims and the colonists that came to the new world soon after them that enabled the building of America was a miracle. It took great faith to establish a new home in a new land. That faith carried on through the next two to three generations as it was no less challenging and difficult to live in the rustic circumstances and environment. Those early years of existence were very difficult, indeed. Survival was a miracle. This is one such story of survival in early colonial times and the *miracle* that accompanied it.

***

"What do ye hear? What is happening yonder?" The mother of three thought to herself as sunrise broke over the freezing February morning in Lancaster, Massachusetts, in 1676. Then fear gripped Mary's heart as she heard the screams of her neighbors, saw the fires, and caught the hollering and yelping of bloodthirsty voices, and the last cries of agony from those being slaughtered. A tribal raiding party had arrived, and the members were executing the colonists.

A little over 50 years after the Mayflower voyage, the Massachusetts Bay Colony rapidly grew. An ever-increasing English population in the region led to colonists encroaching on native Indian lands. Tensions mounted, and war erupted in 1675. In February 1676, during the conflict known as "King Phillip's War," a raiding party comprised of Narragansett, Nipmuc, and Wampanoag warriors descended upon the Puritan settlement of Lancaster in Massachusetts Bay Colony. The swift and brutal attack killed, wounded, or carried many off into captivity. King Phillip's War (1675–1676) pitted the indigenous tribes of New England against the English settlers. King Phillip, whose native name was Metacomet, was the son of the Wampanoag Sachem Massasoit, who established an alliance with the Mayflower Pilgrims. Metacomet took the name Phillip because of the friendly relations between the two groups. However, when Massasoit died and Phillip succeeded him as Sachem, he broke the alliance.

In her personal journal, Mary writes a frightening and tragic personal narrative.

"On the tenth of February 1675, came the Indians with great numbers upon Lancaster: their first coming was about sunrising; several houses were burning, and the smoke ascending to heaven. There were five persons taken in one house; the father, and the mother and a sucking child; they knocked on the head; the other two they took and carried away alive" (Rowlandson 1682, 2).

"… the bullets flying thick, one went through my side, and the same (as would seem) though the bowels and hand of dear child in my arms. My older sisters' children, named William (sic), had then his leg broken, which the Indians perceiving, they knocked him on [his] head" (Rowlandson 1682, 4).

"Of thirty-seven persons who were in this one house, none escaped either present death, or bitter captivity" (Rowlandson 1682, 5).

"It is solemn sight to so many Christians lying in their blood, some here, some there, like accompany of sheep torn by wolves, all of them stripped naked by a company of hellhounds, roaring, singing, ranting, and insulting, as if they would have torn our very hearts out; yet the Lord by His almighty power preserved a number of us from death, for there were twenty-four of us taken alive and carried captive" (Rowlandson 1682, 6).

"There remained nothing to me but one poor wounded babe, and it seemed at present worse than death that it was in such a pitiful condition, bespeaking compassion, and I had no refreshing for it, nor suitable things to revive it" (Rowlandson 1682, 8).

"After this it quickly began to snow, and when night came on, they stopped, and now down I must sit in the snow, by a little fire, and a few boughs behind me, with my sick child in my lap; and calling much for water, being now (through the wound) fallen into a violent fever. My own wound also growing so stiff that I could scarce sit down or rise up; yet so it must be, that I must sit all this cold winter night upon the cold snowy ground, with my sick child in my arms, looking that every hour would be the last of its life; and having no Christian friend near me, either to comfort or help me. Oh, I may see the wonderful power of God, that my spirit did not utterly sink under my affliction: still the Lord upheld me with His gracious and merciful spirit, and were both alive to see the light of the next morning" (Rowlandson 1682, 12).

"Thus, nine days I sat upon my knees, with babe in my lap, till my flesh was raw again; my child being even ready to depart this sorrowful world, they bade me carry it out to another wigwam (I suppose because they would not be troubled with such spectacles) wither I went with a very heavy heart, and down I sat with the picture of death in my lap. About two hours in the night, my sweet babe like a lamb departed this life on Feb. 18, 1675 (76)" (Rowlandson 1682, 15).

Mary Rowlandson and her three children were among the captives. Her daughter Sarah, shot through the hand and abdomen in the attack, died of her wounds after a week of captivity. Mary was separated from her two surviving children and wasn't aware that they were still miraculously alive until a chance meeting with her daughter. Later that same day, her son came to her, but only briefly. For eleven weeks, Mary was forced to accompany the Indians as they made their way across much of New England, evading the English militia. She endured cruelty, beatings, starvation, and freezing temperatures but found the courage to persevere. She was ransomed for twenty pounds and returned to her husband, Joseph Rowlandson. She reunited with her children several weeks later.

Joseph Rowlandson died at Wethersfield, Connecticut, in 1678, and Mary and her children settled in Boston, where she penned and published a narrative of her ordeal in 1682. The Mary Rowlandson captivity narrative is considered the first of what would become a literary genre. The details of her ordeal provide us with a clear look into 17th-century Massachusetts and the troubled relations between English settlers and Native Americans. As depicted in Mary's narrative, the Indians were frequently on the run from the English, often traveling great distances to avoid confrontation. Ultimately, the war devastated the Indigenous peoples of the region.

Patriots, a time for reflection and action.

Critics could argue Mary's survival and release were mere luck combined with a will to live. Perhaps this is so, yet this begs the question. Why did Mary *and* her two elder children survive? It would have been much easier for the tribal members to kill Mary and her remaining children. After all, these captives were a burden to them. The tribal members had to guard, feed, and listen to the annoying and incessant cries of these tortured settlers, not to mention how these captives slowed their movement as they evaded armed settler militias. The tribal Indians had no love or compassion for the settlers, so why not eliminate them? Yet, the tribal leaders did not. The Indians could have enslaved their captors or sold them to other tribes as slaves instead, which was also a common practice. However, the tribe chose to keep and then release Mary and her remaining two children. Through her unwavering faith and deep trust in the miraculous hand of Providence, Mary and her remaining children survived this horrific experience. Clearly, through her own writing, her faith remained unwavering, and she considered her release and the later release of her two children a miraculous event. How can you allow faith to grow to enable miracles to fill your lives, to strengthen and give you hope and direction?

Today, the goodness of the American experience is wrought with turmoil at such a fervent intensity the world has never known. Natural disasters, disease, hatred, violence, the intentional destruction of the bulwarks of society, and the purposeful destruction of our culture are in full force. Abraham Lincoln noted, "If destruction be our lot, we must ourselves be its author and finisher. As a nation of freemen, we must live through all time, or die…" (Lincoln 2018).

How do we, as Americans, combat the imminent threat of our personal destruction and the destruction as a nation?

Practicing gratitude for what you have is an important first step. The next step is to focus your efforts on defining and discovering who you are. Learn your true nature and grow your personal strengths. This concept is powerful as it will help you harden your own personal resolve. For emphasis, to discover your purpose and your personal meaning in life, this act is vital as a citizen and as a being "created in the image of God" (Genesis 1:27 [KJV]). Dr. Jordan Peterson (2018, 85–112) notes in his best-selling work the *12 Rules of Life: An Antidote to Chaos* that a crucial element of living a meaningful life is one should take the time to "compare yourself to who you were yesterday, not to who someone else is today."

Align your life to that discovery, having faith that your discovery will lead to something greater. As you do so, you will connect in deep and meaningful ways with like-minded people who can support you on your journey, especially as you serve and support them. Finally, take consistent, persistent action with a will to survive and thrive. *Then, will the miracles appear.* They will reveal the path before you, removing what may seem to be insurmountable blockers on your personal journey. The miracles may be large, but most often, they will be small. The miracles will be amazing, nonetheless.

These actions build on each other, like the proverbial snowball rolling down a hill that we see in cartoons or in real-life avalanches. At first, the tiny snowball is weak and almost insignificant, sitting on the ledge of a mountain. The snowball is easily melted and evaporated by the heat of the sun in its inert state, or if in the frigid cold, it is merely a useless shape of ice. But a plunge off the ledge to the abundant white, snowy powder below commences the growth of the snowball. It hits a few rocks, shrubs, and trees along its journey, which can be likened to trials, mistakes, and refinement one experiences when doing something hard. However, as the snowball consistently moves, it gets stronger, larger, and more powerful. It connects with other "snowballs" to multiply its power and its purpose. Then an avalanche of change, with positive directed action, awakens and changes the landscape forever. This is the change we need as a nation to preserve, protect, and defend our U.S. Constitution, our Declaration of Independence, the Founders, our history, our heritage, our customs, and our culture and traditions. Discover who you are, take action, and become a purpose-driven, tumbling snowball.

*Figure 4. King Phillips War raid on
a colonial settlement in Massachusetts
(Purchased Alamy.com 23 Sept. 2022)*

*Figure 5. Mary White Rowlandson
carrying wounded infant Sarah after
her capture (Purchased Alamy.com
23 Sept. 2022)*

An Epoch Signing—The Declaration of Independence

Honor the U.S. Declaration of Independence &
Founding Fathers

(Take Courage in Supporting Liberty)

*M*om, I don't want to go!" cried the tear-stained seven-year-old boy while sitting in the black plastic passenger seat of the 1973 yellow Volkswagen Beetle. He had never participated in a team sport before. He never had to "battle" on a field against another team. He did not even know how to play soccer. He was afraid of the other boys. Would they accept him? Would they bully or make fun of him? He protested; he felt like his personal choice in this matter was of no concern.

However, the boy's mother knew signing him up for the sport was the right thing to do for a host of reasons. She decided to use this moment to teach an important life lesson. "I understand how you feel, but I already signed you up and paid for the program. In life, you sometimes have to do things you do not like, even if you fear it. You may find yourself in a position of no choice. The only choice you then have is to work through it, learn, and do your very best. Life is not fair. Now, get out of the car, go meet your teammates, and make new friends."

The colonists and the Founding Fathers also found themselves in a position of having no options. And they too greatly feared. Have you ever felt deep knots in your stomach with a foreboding sense of fear? Have you ever risked everything, including your freedom, your life, your liberties, your family, and your property, with the hope of something larger than yourself? Have you ever risked it all for a cause? Perhaps we are living in such times where extreme courage is necessary, as it was in the story below.

✻✻✻

The summer heat simmered the city. Thick humidity in bustling Philadelphia added a moist layer onto the already thick attire the men wore, and on their tired and wary foreheads. For days, cramped in a small room—the closed windows prevented passersby's from eavesdropping and kept pesky flies out—a group of men solemnly met to ratify an epoch document. Nothing so eloquent or declarative like it had been written before. The document called for divorce.

Its opening paragraphs proclaimed:

"The unanimous Declaration of the 13 united States of America, When in the Course of human events, it becomes necessary for one people to dissolve the political bands which have connected it to another, and to assume among the powers of the earth, the separate and equal station to which the Laws of Nature and Nature's God entitle them, a decent respect to the opinions of mankind requiring that they should declare the cause which impels them to this separation."

"We hold these truths to be self-evident, that all men are created equal. That they are endowed by their Creator with unalienable Rights, that among these are Life, Liberty, and the pursuit of Happiness.—*That to secure these Rights, Governments are instituted among Men, deriving their just powers from the consent of the governed,*—That whenever any Form of Government becomes destructive of these ends, it is the Right of the People to alter or abolish it and to institute new Government, laying its foundation on such principles and organizing its powers in such form, as to them shall seem most likely to affect their Safety and Happiness" (Jefferson 2012, 108).

A stunning, monumental document, indeed. Yet, it was also treasonous. Dr. Benjamin Rush (1811) of Pennsylvania recalled when Elbridge Gerry of Massachusetts signed it.

"Do you recollect *the pensive and awful silence* which pervaded the house where we were called up, one after the other, to the President of Congress, to subscribe to what we believe by many at the time to be our death warrants. The Silence and gloom of the morning were interrupted, I recollect only for a moment by Col: Harrison of Virginia, who said to Mr. Gerry at the table, 'I shall have a great advantage over you Mr. Gerry when we are all hung for what we are now doing. From the size and weight of my body, I shall die in a few minutes, but from the lightness of your body you will dance in the air an hour or two before you are dead.' This speech procured a transient smile, but it was soon succeeded by the Solemnity with which the whole business was conducted."

Patriots, a time for reflection and action.

Today, like our forefathers, you are called to courageous, solemn action to get personally and directly involved. Your duty is significantly more than casual voting. It is participatory politics. It is *citizenship*. The Yankee patriot, Noah Webster, noted, "If the citizens neglect their duty and place unprincipled men in office, the government will soon be corrupted ... If a republican government fails to secure public prosperity and happiness, it must be because the citizens neglect the Divine commands, and elect bad men to make and administer the laws." (Straub 2012). This is our state of affairs today. To course correct this terrible reality that faces our nation this very hour, you are called to get involved at a deeper, more meaningfully important level. It may produce a sense of fear and cause your stomach to knot. However, the most important virtue, courage, starts with you. Your courage will inspire others.

Reclaim your citizenship voice and do your duties. What is a citizen? In his work titled *The Dying Citizen*, Dr. Victor Davis Hansen (2021) provides a classic American definition. A citizen is "an individual with the ability to influence the political, social, and economic systems the regime in which they live, under a *fully* consensual government, and with constitutionally protected freedoms." That is a lot of responsibility. This articulates how each citizen has a vital role to fulfill in the Republic.

You are governed by your consent, with protected rights that should also be vigorously understood and defended. This responsibility gives credence to Dr. Benjamin Franklin's quip, "[You have] a Republic, if you can keep it" (Miller 2022). Foregoing or relinquishing these obligations to a detached political body is dangerous.

There are many who would gladly take liberty from you, such as unaccountable administrative bureaucracies, corporations, and unelected bodies like the United Nations, the Gates Foundation, the World Economic Forum, or BlackRock— all filled with ideas contrary to freedom and agency. Your citizenship cannot be casually taken or given away without dire consequences to your protected freedoms. Notice how those in power do not like this traditional meaning of citizenship and use forceful words and actions to compel compliance. For example, note how agents of "justice"— so-called "law enforcement"—"tag" parents for attending and vocally speaking at school board meetings (Malcolm 2021). Notice the intertwining of the above entities to include other technology and governmental agencies that actively suppress free speech and collude together to affect election outcomes. Look no further than the recent revelations regarding the largest and most influential technology companies.

The mask is completely off; our adversary has been fully revealed! We have been here before! What are you going to do to ensure that FREEDOM and LIBERTY remain in this land? Do not be afraid; take courage. President George Washington wisely observed, and you see before your own eyes, "Truth will ultimately prevail where there is pains to bring it to light" (Washington 1794).

"I don't have time!" might be your refrain. Consider we are all stretched for time. But is FREEDOM not worth the fight? Those who have sought to take away your freedoms and to change your customs, culture, and tradition lead busy lives too. Yet, with religious fervor, they find the time—and behold the fruit of their destruction! By failing to do your obligations in the struggle, you are signing something—you are signing away your freedoms and your natural rights. Remember, too, as Thomas Jefferson wrote the stunning draft of the Declaration of Independence, he experienced extreme personal hardships. Jefferson and his wife suffered the passing of four of their six children, and after 10 years of marriage, his wife passed away. Jefferson described her death as his having lost "the cherished companion of my life" ("Brief Biography of Thomas Jefferson" 2022). Yet, Jefferson found the time to propel the Glorious Cause forward through his belief in the individual, his reasoned intellect, and his pen.

How do you reclaim and protect your citizenship? While voting is extremely important, your vote does not matter if an illegal vote cancels it out or the unscrupulous cheat the system. Learn about what living and supporting the Republic means. Consider becoming a Precinct Committee Officer or a Block Captain in your local area. Consider becoming a poll watcher to ensure fraud is caught and challenged. Consider running for office yourself, perhaps for your local town or county council. Be on the school board. Vocally call and take legal action for the elimination of federal and state agencies and other bureaucracies that seek to oppress or that have failed or abused their power. But act, for inaction results in a barren farmland field; it will not produce a great harvest without effort!

Participate in events with loved ones and children that celebrate the greatness of America. Teach them why our customs, culture, and traditions matter. Take time, ideally with your family, to participate in and understand the issues of your day. Talk about the issues that beset us and have healthy and spirited debates within the home.

Further, cease electing unprincipled and career politicians who enrich themselves for years.

If you do not stand now, you will be sitting in your sunset years asking, "How did it all go wrong?"

It is never time to stop fighting for freedom, and it is never time to panic. It is NEVER time to despair. A new age is dawning, and you are invited and needed in this Glorious Cause that started with our forefathers and continues to this day. Thomas Paine wrote, "Heaven knows how to put a proper price upon its goods; and it would be strange indeed if so celestial an article as FREEDOM should not be highly rated" (Paine 2012).

The costs for not acting are too high. You see the costs of inaction around you. Too many have sacrificed for our freedoms, and too much blood and treasure has been spilt to let it be casually thrown aside by forces that want to impose their will on you.

Finally, consider this, "To those fifty-six who signed there was great personal future significance ... Nine signers died of wounds or hardships during the Revolutionary War. Five were captured or imprisoned, in some cases with brutal treatment. The wives, sons, and daughters of others were killed, jailed, mistreated, or left penniless ... The houses of twelve signers were burned to the ground. Seventeen lost everything they owned ... Their fortunes were forfeit, but their honor was not. NO SIGNER DEFECTED ..." (Davis 2022).

Figure 6. The signing of the Declaration of Independence, 1776

(Purchased Alamy.com 23 Sept. 2022)

Sovel Beshvil a Ahalom & Atzmaot / Hofesh

(Hebrew for Suffering for Peace & Liberty)

*Honor the U.S. Declaration of Independence &
Founding Fathers*

**(Discover Who You Are & Add Your Unique
Talents to the Cause of Liberty)**

o you like being recognized for a job well done?
Most of us do. When you show a commitment to a
cause or a belief or serve others and keep your word, it brings
the respect of others and enhances your stature in their eyes.
It's rewarding to hear friends, family, employers, or respected
co-workers say, in effect, "Send for (your name)" because they
trust in your experience, your wisdom, and your abilities,
and they believe your word. This is especially true if you are
somehow perceived as different or lacking, yet you show
devotion, dedication, duty, and loyalty all the same, using
your personal talents to great effect. This is the true story of
one such legend.

✳✳✳

The excited stranger disembarked the sailing vessel. Growing up poor in a refugee family in 1700s Poland, he learned the ways of Europe to survive. A studious, trusted, and honest young man, Haym cultured valuable skills. He became particularly adept at business, learning multiple languages, finance, and other international commerce skills of his day. After his travels throughout Western Europe, the now-wealthy businessman returned to Poland only to find his homecoming would be short-lived. The great European powers of the day forced Haym to leave his land of birth. Shortly thereafter, the 32-year-old found himself in London. Sensing opportunity, he departed London, sailing to the colonies in 1775 to New York City to establish a brokerage business. A stranger in this new land indeed, Haym Salomon was devout to his Jewish faith, surrounded by many who practiced Christianity.

The fires of liberty sparked Haym's mind and bosom nearly as soon as his shoes touched the new world shores. Haym quickly caught the vision of what the United States of America could be. The land teemed with prosperity, its landscape blessed with its new barns, lively communities, and farmland of ample corn and grain. He came when the battle of Lexington in Massachusetts turned the conflict with England into a "hot" war. Haym arrived in time to see and hear the rhetorical debates that raged in statehouses and publications— like Thomas Paine's Common Sense—on whether to support Massachusetts or remain loyal to the British crown.

To Haym's delight, the Continental Congress fully ratified the Declaration of Independence on July 4, 1776—the document to divorce their British overseers. He supported the patriot cause with fervor, even becoming a member of the Sons of Liberty in 1776. Alas, his active support for independence eventually landed him in a British prison as a spy with a death sentence on his head.

Fortunately, Haym's sharp mind and multi-lingual abilities came in handy. Using his fluent German language skills, he successfully convinced—in part by bribing with gold coins— the German Hessian guard to help him escape (1894, 7–8). After his escape from the prison in New York City, he moved his family to Philadelphia to the heart of the Glorious Cause.

Haym's contribution to the cause of liberty cannot be understated; for the Glorious Cause laid financially in tatters. The Continental Congress sluggishly approved scarce funds. Haym Saloman, working directly with Robert Morris, a Founding Father and the movement's Superintendent of Finance, financed the Cause to provide pay, arms, rations, uniforms, and supplies to the Continental troops. Using his finely honed, unique skills, Haym brokered many transactions with Holland and France and personally loaned $650,000 ($20,000,000 in 2022 dollars) to fund the Continental Army and Navy. When the clarion call came from his blossoming country, Haym answered that call with the talents and gifts he had been blessed with. While he did not possess the skills and knowledge of the art of warfare and arms, his financial genius and skills at brokering deals and finding funds were a godsend. In fact, Haym's vital skills in the closing days of the War for Independence were invaluable (Peters 1911).

As General George Washington's troops marched to the besieged community of Yorktown, Virginia, the General had a serious problem—he exhausted his war chest! So close to defeating an exceptionally capable foe, General Lord Charles Cornwallis, the Continental Army and Navy lacked money. His hungry, unhappy troops threatened mutiny. Washington, exchanging multiple letters with Robert Morris, urgently requested funds between August 17, 1781 and October 19, 1781, even asking for rum to lift the spirits of the unpaid troops (Washington, 1781). Morris consistently replied the treasury was empty and he was working on it.

It is difficult to find the original source, but legend has it that General Washington or members of Congress, in desperate need, thought of Haym Salomon, and asked Morris to contact him (Kaufman 2022). A year after the Battle of Yorktown ended, Robert Morris noted in his August 26, 1782 journal entry that he recalled he "sent for Salomon and desired for him to raise money…" and two days later, "Salomon, the broker, came and I urged him to leave no stone unturned to find out money and the means by which I can obtain it" (Peters 1911, 18–19). Thus, people began to say, "Send for Haym Salomon."

Haym reportedly responded quickly, raising $20,000 ($460,000 in 2022 dollars). He possibly loaned some personal funds for immediate use (Peters 1911, 19). His financial acumen and his strong working relationship with the Minister of France—and possibly through unofficial back-channels with the Kingdom of Spain—directly contributed to the British Army's defeat at Yorktown and, by extension, the war (Morris 1973, 122–123).

After the war, Haym continued to help suffering war veterans and his local community, raising funds to build a historic synagogue in Philadelphia and serving as a treasurer at a local Jewish charitable organization (Kaufman 2022).

Sadly, Hyam died from an illness acquired while in the New York prison, leaving his family penniless.

Hyam's obituary in the Independent Gazetteer read:

> Thursday, last, expired, after a lingering illness, Mr. Haym Salomon, an eminent broker of this city, was a native of Poland, and of the Hebrew nation. He was remarkable for his skill and integrity in his profession, and for his generous and humane deportment. His remains were yesterday deposited in the burial ground of the synagogue of this city (Kaufman 2022).

His children were left without an inheritance. However, we as a nation are fortunate to have a man of Jewish descent sacrificed so much for the inheritance that we now enjoy.

Patriots, a time for reflection and action.

Haym deeply experienced the "old world" as a young man learning his craft. His multi-lingual abilities, moderation, courage, and marvelous success in Europe demonstrate he had the trustworthiness, integrity, habits, mind, discipline, and attitude to become something more in spite of his humble background and heritage. Haym lacked skills in the arts of war, nor did he possess tremendous rhetorical abilities. However, in the hope of America, he saw more opportunities than he ever experienced in Europe. He very literally gave all to the cause of freedom because he believed in it so passionately, not just for himself, but for his family and his fellow countryman too. Haym could have easily sat on the sidelines with his wealth and become a neutral party to the War for Independence in New York City. He could have supported the British Crown, who, by experience, numbers, training, and skill, should have easily prevailed against the colonists. A common-sense businessman and a shady bet-keeping "bookie" alike would both agree betting on the British was a better choice. However, Haym did not. He used the talents he had, his unique and important skills, which you are the beneficiaries of today.

Find your talent and develop it. But you may ask, what do I have to give? The discovery is a vital, personal journey of discovery. Intuitively, one knows where their passions lie and how to make those talents of use. Some discover this early, but for most of us, it takes time and deep reflection, much prayer or meditation, and trial and error to figure this out.

To aid and inspire you, there is a parable on the richness of blessings and discovering your talents that perhaps you've heard. The following parable demonstrates the stewardship we are all given over our lives and that one day, we will be called to account for our life's actions. This is true regardless of your spiritual background or belief. Many believe they will be accountable to their Creator; others may simply be accountable to themselves, asking in their later years, "What did I do to make this world a better place?" This connects you to *logos*, word and truth. Please note the growth that happens when you take action. The parable:

Before a long journey away, a Master called his servants. To one, he gave five talents (a talent being a silver or gold coin, but a flair, gift, knack, or special ability for this writing's purpose also applies), to another servant, two talents, and a third, one talent, with a charge to increase what they had been given. The servant with five increased their talents to 10, and the servant with two talents increased to four. However, the servant given one talent hid it. When the good Master returned and required an account, he blessed and congratulated the two servants who increased their talents and promised those good and faithful servants more responsibilities and more blessings in his kingdom. To the one servant who hid their talent, that servant proclaimed, "I was afraid...I hid the talent." The Master, incredulously, could not understand how the gift and charge he gave was so summarily dismissed. How crushing, how disappointing when the servant had something wonderful to grow, yet hid his talent. The good Master chided and took away that one talent and removed the unprofitable servant from the kingdom with an admonition for all of us. "For unto every one that hath shall be given, and he shall have abundance:

but from him that hath not shall be taken away even that which he hath" (Matthew 25:14–29 [KJV]).

What are your talents?

May your Creator enlighten your mind and soul with the talents they have blessed you with and so rightly wish to bless you with. This knowledge is required so that you can develop it and use it to serve for good, wise, and righteous purposes.

May those of you with *leadership* talents be blessed with the talents of General George Washington, whose steadfast leadership in the most difficult times kept the Glorious Cause alive.

May those of you with a knack for the *written word* be blessed with the talents of Thomas Jefferson, whose eloquent pen gave birth to a nation and defeated a great empire.

May those of you with skills in *speech and rhetoric* be blessed with the oratory talents of Patrick Henry, whose impassioned phrase, "Give me Liberty or give me Death," is a motto for the ages.

May those of you with *intellect and wisdom* be blessed with the talents of Dr. Benjamin Franklin, whose wisdom, pursuit of personal growth, scientific mind, and statesmanship gave gravitas to the Glorious Cause, drew respect from other nations, and produced inventions and ideas that serve us well to this day.

And if there be one talent, important above all, let us ALL develop the *courage* of Samuel Adams. Samuel Adams's courage and ability to bring people together for positive action sparked, bonded and breathed life into these United

States of America, created the Declaration, and set forth the foundation for the Bill of Rights.

Please ask yourself, "What do I have to give to the cause of Freedom?" True citizenship requires such development and responsibility. Converse with loved and trusted ones and figure out how you or your family can be engaged to strengthen the bulwarks of freedom and society. We all have our unique talents. Combine your talents with virtue, and you will be unstoppable. What can you give when your country's clarion call sounds as it is right now? For the Founders want to say today, "Send for (insert your name)."

Figure 7. Haym Saloman (25 OCT 2022)

The Flag & Sergeant William Jasper

Stand for Old Glory

(Live Pieatas-Patriotism. Why Old Glory's Symbolism Is Important)

The 10-year-old boy and his little brother displayed great excitement about the event. Their exuberance manifested itself as the two barely controlled, energetic boys jumped up and down with anticipation. They asked their parents a host of questions to help them understand what to expect. After all, this was their first parade! But this was not just any parade. Mom and Dad took them to a local, New England town's 4th of July Parade. On this hot summer morning, hundreds of people lined up along the street. Red, white, and blue banners, American flags, Betsy Ross flags, and buntings decorated the beautiful small-town scene. Cars carrying veterans and local dignitaries streamed by. Music from marching bands in colorful uniforms played snappy tunes with pretty girls in beautiful costumes throwing batons and streaming flags dancing to the tunes. Firemen in trucks, old and new, sounded their sirens and flashed their strobe lights, and, best of all, threw out candy to the kids! Police and military members in uniform proudly paraded by, chests up, displaying strength, confidence, and purpose. The crowds cheered for these community heroes and country, leaving a deep impression on the young boys. Celebrating America was important to their parents; perhaps it should be important for the brothers too.

Why do we stand for the American flag? What does it represent? The American flag is a symbol of the Faith, Family, and Liberty we enjoy on this blessed land. However, early during the Cause, what is known as the Betsy Ross flag, with its 13 stripes and 13 stars in a circle, did not exist. Various colonies had standards that represented their colonies and individual territories and regiments. Nonetheless, each banner and its standard bearers served as an important inspiration to many, and directly contributed to winning the Glorious Cause. Their individual flags represented their neighbors and their community. Further, standard bearers were crucial in the war; they moved troops and regiments forward, and they were also vital to morale. Standard bearers were also very brave as they became an easy target for enemy fire. If a standard-bearer fell, confusion in the ranks at the falling of a standard-bearer could quickly turn victory into sure defeat. Here is a story of one such standard bearer, who, while not well known, did his small but vital part to support the Cause.

***

BOOM! BOOM! BOOM! The British ship's thundering cannon bombarded the South Carolina hastily-made fort of earth and spongy palmetto logs, producing flying splinters of dirt in wood. The Second South Carolina regiment, a band of local militia, fortified Sullivan's Island, a small but important piece of ground outside the mouth of Charleston Harbor. Coming off of winter, the ground laid muddy and wet in the spring of 1776. The war that started a year ago in Lexington, Massachusetts, now made its way south to a region deeply divided over a conflict with its parent country. Unlike the Northern Colonies, where more colonists felt the oppression of British rule and therefore developed a strong distaste for its oppressive tactics, colonists in South Carolina did not experience the harsh treatment. This difference resulted in bitter divisions among the populace of the colony. Tories, supporters of the Crown, and Patriots were nearly evenly divided in South Carolina over the prospect of American independence. That spring, British General Sir Henry Clinton and Royal Navy Admiral Sir Peter Parker launched an expedition to the south with the aim of securing a port and base of operations. Wilmington, North Carolina, was the original destination, but bad weather and logistical problems forced them to focus their efforts on Charleston. One of England's jewel cities, Charleston boasted a great harbor and easy access to the West Indies for commerce. Charleston prosperous port traded molasses, tobacco, rum, and textile material in the British mercantile system. The city served as a fine naval port as well.

Among Colonial Colonel William Moultrie's Second South Carolina Regiment was a backcountry immigrant to South Carolina, a 26-year-old man named William Jasper. Where he came from—Virginia, Pennsylvania, or another colony—is not known. What is known is William Jasper joined a Grenadier company in 1775 to support the Glorious Cause. Now, here Jasper fought, at Sullivan Island, with dirt and palmetto debris flying around him as the deafening roar of battle played out.

About midday, Admiral Parker moved several of his ships to within a few hundred meters of the fort, concentrating their broadsides on the fort's parapet. Meanwhile, Colonel Moultrie grew alarmed that his regiment was running out of ammunition. As the British assault intensified, a crowd of anxious observers gathered on the waterfront in Charleston. Troop and colonial morale in the fort and in Charleston sank. Wanting to make every shot count, Colonel Moultrie ordered his men to return fire only when the British ships paused for reloading. This not only conserved ammunition but also gave the Americans time to aim their shots well. The colonists badly damaged several British ships.

As the ferocity of the battle began to peak, the Fort Sullivan flag, planted on the fort's parapet, was suddenly hit by a shell and fell outside the fort. With morale already low, Sergeant Jasper swung into action. With cannon balls exploding all around him, Jasper leaped over the parapet and recovered the regimental flag. Securing it to a swabbing pole, Jasper stood on the parapet holding the flag until a more permanent fixture could be set in place. Inspired by this act of selfless courage, the men of the Second Regiment fought on with an intensified resolve. As the daylight waned, the British conceded defeat and returned north. Charleston was saved, at least for the time being.

William Jasper's heroic act inspired his comrades to stay the course, ultimately securing victory. South Carolina President, John Rutledge, commended Jasper for what he had done by giving him his own sword and offering him a lieutenant's commission, which Jasper declined. In the coming years, Colonel Moultrie relied heavily on Jasper in the fight against the British. Sgt Jasper did so until he succumbed to wounds sustained while leading a charge in the battle for Savanah, Georgia, in October 1779, but doing so only after grabbing the regimental flag from a fallen soldier, inspiring his unit to charge forward in the face of imminent danger (Schoolfield 1976, 14).

Patriots, a time for reflection and action.

There is a well-known story that members of the Church of Jesus Christ of Latter-day Saints learn in their religious tradition. The story is about a leader named Moroni who held the title "Captain," in essence a high-ranking general. A deeply religious and righteous man, he hated the shedding of blood. Yet, he lived in a time of deep divisions and contention in his land. The political class achieved power through deception using much flattery of words, the perversion of law, corruption of judges, and targeted assassination of political rivals through secret designs. They aimed to conquer all the lands, subjugate the people, and install their scheming leader as king. The people pleaded for Moroni to head the armies in defense. In prayerful thought and humility, he reflected on how he could inspire his countrymen and his troops in the upcoming battle between his forces and the treacherous foe. Through inspiration, he created a standard from his torn coat and wrote on it, "In memory of our God, our religion, and freedom, and our peace, our wives, and our children," and attached it to a pole (Pratt 1830, 322–325). His troops bowed to the makeshift flag in reverence and allegiance and carried it that day in the battle and subsequent bloody war that followed. That simple but powerful phrase made all the difference to his army. Moroni's efforts inspired *pieatas*.

"*Pieatas*" is a Latin root word for Patriotism, a virtue that in many circles is disdained today. However, this beautiful word, Pieatas, attaches to it a deep, heartfelt, significant obligation and responsibility from a citizen within their heart and soul to demonstrate *fidelis agape* (faithful love) to their faith and community. This obligation means a devoted but obedient duty to God (or one's religion/faith), an affectionate duty to one's neighbor and/or family, and faithful love and defense of country—in that order. This obligation forever binds them to their home, anchoring them to the place they love. That familiar obligation to God, family, and country used to be commonplace. Today, *pieatas* desperately needs to be revived.

Catholic Arch-Bishop Fulton Sheen, a powerful, award-winning American presence on television in the 1950s to 1970s, aptly noted in his *Quo Vadis, America* (Where are you going, America?) television presentation that with regards to these three pillars of *pieatas*, "When one goes out, all go out" (Catholic Chroma Channel 2020, 0:24:32). When one is extinguished, they all extinguish. Is this not what we see today? Are we witnessing a clear attempt to change America's culture, customs, and traditions to disassociate the past from the present to create a new but ultimately destructive future?

How do we know it is destructive? We know because we have seen it fail before in the fall of ancient Rome, the demise of ancient Greece, the end of Alexander the Great's Macedonian empire, the ruin of Carthage, and the collapse of ancient Persia and Jerusalem.

We also know because recent history reveals it too. Indeed, the theories of Karl Marx, as championed by men such as Vladimir Lenin and Joseph Stalin of Russia, Fidel Castro of Cuba, Pol Pot of Cambodia, Ho Chi Minh of Vietnam, Mao Zedong of China, and Kim-Il Sung of North Korea tells how they usurped power, and the tragic consequences for humanity that followed. These adherents to Marxism lied, divided, conquered, and killed their opponents—even those ideologically aligned with them—in the quest for absolute power and control, while personally amassing fortunes for themselves. This resulted in tens of millions of people killed by forced labor, death camps, forced military conscription, starvation, and torture in the 20th century alone. If one did not tolerate their rule or lies and spoke out, they disappeared—permanently.

Today, observe the openly Marxist and corrupt influence of groups who promote Critical Race Theory. The theory divides folks into the "oppressor" and "oppressed" class, yet actually destroy or harm those they purport to stand up for. We also know because we clearly see the division, hate, and destruction it is bearing in the United States and Europe. We see its fruits. One needs to look no further than secretive cells of dark-hooded Antifa who threaten, fight, harm, and even kill in the name of Antifascism, yet ironically use fascist tactics to advance their vile agenda.

Study the devious yet transparent plans of the World Economic Forum for creating a global society. Remember the World Health Organization's quick and vocal protection and support of the Chinese Communist Party, the cabal who unleashed a biological weapon known as COVID-19 (by accident or on purpose, we will never know). Note the strident demonization and subsequent defunding of honest, local law enforcement—our own community members—resulting in uncontrolled crime in once great cities and communities. Witness the persistent and strident attempts to equate or outright replace the Stars and Stripes with fascist inspired, darkened streamers, or distinct multicolored banners of rebellion, rejecting Old Glory as a symbol of a bygone era. The destructive pattern is merely repeating itself.

Indeed, we have we seen this before, and we are living through it again!

Now, imagine, if you would, a mosaic that combines all the regimental, colonial, and state flags together in a grand piece of art. One cannot help to be in awe of the masterpiece. In total, these flags in the artistic mosaic are Old Glory. It represents *all* of us. In aggregate, it is a mosaic of citizens, lovers of liberty, and defenders of their faith, their communities and families, and their country, independent spirit, and Constitution. We stand for the American Flag during the anthem in reverence and remembrance. We remember the dreamers and their accomplishments. We reflect on families, workers, and statesmen who bound together to create a Nation. We ponder hard-fought rights, charity, liberties, battles, wars, veterans, and those that died to defend our God-given freedoms for our religion, peace, and families from enemies within and without. We stand recognizing the imperfections of the nation but strive, in the words of the U.S. Constitution, to form a "more perfect union" (U.S. Constitution, preamble). *Standing for the flag is a sacred act.*

Well-known celebrities who kneel during the anthem, burn, turn their backs, or refuse to stand for the Stars and Stripes argue that their personal grievances from perceived or real wrongs warrant a form of protest to bring attention to *their personal cause.* However, while their selfish protest and actions are an attempt to *denigrate their nation, flag, and, ultimately, you, they are only denigrating themselves.* While they have the right to voluntarily separate themselves from this custom and courtesy, the hard truth is *with great pride and hubris,* they set themselves up as someone who knows better, is superior to you, is more enlightened, and then snubs the very nation's unifying symbol of a free nation that provided them the opportunity to succeed. They are ungrateful. They are myopically selfish. Many are spoiled and are exceptionally soft in the luxuries of life this nation has, in great measure, created. Why should you give credence and support such behavior?

It is time to permanently turn off the professional sports channels and refuse to watch ungrateful millionaires play while "Rome burns"—i.e., our nation falls. Stop buying their paraphernalia and cease purchasing expensive shoes and other garments that support the unappreciative. Why use your hard-earned dollars to reward companies that do not support meaningful values, customs, cultures, and traditions? The same sports figures who angrily and ignorantly decry America's slave past quickly turn a blind eye to products made by forced labor embraced by the Chinese Communist Party or the illicit human-slave and sex trafficking conducted by the foreign and cruel drug cartels at the Southern Border of the United States. Further, it is time to stop buying certain sports magazines. These periodicals formerly revered athleticism, physical fitness and health but now are mere rags that have traded truth and reason in an effort to support an ideology in the name of "inclusion" to promote unflattering health and lifestyles.

Instead, form or participate in local sporting activities with your children, families, and neighbors. In the process, teach and engage your families and neighbors about the nation's flag and *pieatas*, its meaning, and its importance. Do so at a local little league baseball or high school football game. Go on trail hikes, play games, bowl, bike ride, sing the patriotic songs, and reflect on the blessings those before you have bestowed upon you. Instead of wearing a jersey with some sports figure's name on the back, wear one with *your family's name on the back.* Like Sgt William Jasper and Moroni, build and hoist proudly into the sky your own family's personal standard, and remember who you are, what is important, and what you are willing to stand for, to include Old Glory.

Figure 8. Moultry Flag flown at Fort Sullivan (https://www.crwflags.com/ FOTW/FLAGS/us-moul.html)

Figure 9. Second South Carolina Regiment Flag (https://www.crwflags. com/page0660sc2ndregiment1775. html)

"I Cannot Live Without Books" -Thomas Jefferson

Believe in Education & Critical Thinking, Not Indoctrination

(Read, Learn, Educate Via the Lens of Truth, Reason, & Virtue)

*L*earning never ended at home. Mom, being a teacher, did not want her two boys' brains to go stale during the three-month summer recess. So, she required her sons to practice regular mathematics and reading drills. Multiplication tables, addition, division, and subtraction became a regular routine set before the boys. "No learning, no play" seemed to be her motto to her seemingly tortured sons, who longed to be outside in the summer sun. Further, she took her sons on trips to the local library to pick out books for summer reading with the expectation of a report on what they learned before the end of the summer. The boys bellyached at this extra "school" work. But her wisdom in keeping their minds sharp and proactively thinking served them well throughout their lives.

Like the boys' mother, the Founding Fathers were men of great intellect and wisdom too. Indeed, they understood that an educated mind is truly a free mind. It is time to learn to free our minds and engage in the battle of ideas and liberty. Let the following story inspire you to the virtue of wisdom and life-long learning.

**

The citizens of the young nation stood shocked. Its beautiful new capital building laid engulfed in thick black smoke wafting in the air and choking those who breathed the noxious breeze—the emerging city of the young Republic destroyed and gleefully pillaged. To add to the destruction, British troops in the late summer of 1814 also destroyed Congress' library and its nearly 3,000 volumes. These books, invaluable volumes, supported the legislative body to inform their thinking toward the creation of the new nation's laws. Total losses amounted to approximately $13,000 in 1814, a hefty sum amounting to nearly $205,000 in today's currency. However, the loss of wisdom and ideas was incalculable.

Thomas Jefferson, the former U.S. president, departed Washington DC, stepping down from politics only six years before to retire to his beloved Monticello in Virginia. Jefferson's love of learning and books was well known. He was considered a renaissance man of his age. He intensely worried at such a loss of treasure. Distressed at this turn of events, Jefferson wrote to his friend, Samuel Harrison Smith, a federal commissioner, asking him to deliver a letter to Congress. The letter offered to sell the former president's personal collection at whatever price the U.S. Congress saw fit ("Thomas Jefferson" 2022). After much debate, Congress accepted the offer, purchasing Jefferson's 6,487 volumes at a price of $23,950, or $376,000 in today's currency. Jefferson cataloged and parted with his collection of books to rebuild what is now known as the Library of Congress.

The Founding Fathers understood that the Republic could not exist, thrive, or survive if its Congress and the general populace it represented were not personally informed, educated, and knowledgeable critical thinkers. The destruction of the first library represented a destruction of the right to learn, to gain wisdom, and to free the mind from chains of tyranny. Benjamin Rush noted, "It is favourable to liberty. Freedom can exist only in the society of knowledge. Without learning, men are incapable of knowing their rights, and where learning is confined to a few people, liberty can be neither equal nor universal" (Jewell 2011). Samuel Adams penned, "While the People are virtuous, they cannot be subdued; but when once they lose their Virtue, they will be ready to surrender their Liberties to the first external or *internal* Invader ... If virtue and knowledge are diffused among the People, they will never be enslav'd. This will be their great Security" (Adams 1908, 123–124). Wrote Thomas Jefferson, "Enlighten the people generally, and tyranny and oppressions of body and mind will vanish like evil spirits at the dawn of the day" (Jefferson 1816).

Critics claim Jefferson's reasons for selling were more selfish; he needed the funds. It is true that he sold his volumes, in part, because he needed the money to pay off debts ("Sale of Book" & "Debt" 2022). But in the larger scheme, he demonstrated a grand commitment to wisdom, classical education, and learning to the new republic. Indeed, he stayed true to his values that learning, critical thinking, and enlightenment were virtuous principles that needed fostering and growth if the new Republic were to succeed.

Writing to his friend Mr. Smith, Jefferson noted, "An interesting treasure is added to your city, now become the depository of unquestionably the choicest collection of books in the U.S., and I hope it will not be without some general effect on the literature of our country" ("Thomas Jefferson" 2022). Many of the original collection of Thomas Jefferson's books still grace the halls of the Library of Congress in a special room. The room is a testament to his luminous learning on a host of subjects. His cultured mind had a voracious appetite for ideas and discovery. Thomas Jefferson spoke multiple languages, and he was skilled in mathematics, geometry, calculus, as well as philosophy. He understood and learned modern and ancient history.

Further, Jefferson played a role in creating the splendid monumental library in the wake of this national 1814 tragedy. Today, the grand Library of Congress with its beauty parallels the European grand cathedrals and churches. In fact, it's designed much like a church. Its stunning halls, murals, paintings, and sculptures very much resemble renaissance era art and beauty. The Library of Congress today stands as a monument to Jefferson's sacrifice, inwardly and outwardly. Alas, Jefferson painfully gave up these volumes; it was akin to giving up his children. As the last of 10 horse-drawn carts of books lumbered away by carriage to Washington, DC, along bumpy and dusty early American dirt roads, he mourned in writing to his fellow patriot John Adams, *"I Cannot Live Without Books"* (Jefferson 1815).

Patriots, a time for reflection and action.

In ancient times, learning wisdom and ancient truths via a classical, liberal arts education served a noble purpose. That purpose was to produce a citizenry of thoughtful, intellectually wise, and powerful individuals who could do their part in building and maintaining a peaceful and prosperous society. It sought to impart the virtues of wisdom, leadership, temperance, justice, and courage to develop good character. Virtuous education integrates these traits with honorable customs, cultures, and traditions to not only help the individual but bind the community in a common purpose to develop a culture. Virtuous learning connects to the Divine and, with free agency and thought, enables one to recognize purpose and meaning in their own life and profoundly understand how one's life truly connects to the lives of others. Why does the classic 1940s Jimmy Stewart movie "It's a Wonderful Life" capture our hearts during the Christmas season? The reason is that the movie reminds us of these eternal, virtuous truths.

Paideia is a Greek word the ancients used for "education." However, the English translation of "education" woefully describes the depth of the word's meaning. Classically speaking, *paideia* means the rearing or development of the young, building their beliefs and forming their understanding of culture from toddler to teenager. This is when the young minds are most perceptive and receptive to understanding culture, tradition, obligation, faith, and the importance of family and community. However, Pete Hegseth and David Goodwin (2022) insightfully argue in their literary work *Battle for the American Mind, Uprooting of a Century of Miseducation* that American children's *paideia* has been radically altered for the last five generations. Today's *paideia* denigrates traditional American values and detaches a child from American culture, family, and tradition.

There is ample evidence to support these claims. Videos show school administrators and teachers openly admitting to influencing children to destructive indoctrination that is not in harmony with parents' or the nation's founding values. Numerous concerned parents complained with alarm as they learned teachers told kids to not talk to their parents about topics like globalism, Critical Race Theory, climate change, and topics related to gender and sexuality. As renowned classical scholar Dr. Steve Turley observed, when was the last time you heard about a school promoting American values and American citizenship as opposed to being a good Global citizen (Turley 2022)?

Writing to his son, John Quincy Adams, John Adams noted, "In Company with Sallust, Cicero, Tacitus and Livy, you will learn Wisdom and Virtue. You will see them represented, with all the Charms which Language and Imagination can exhibit, and Vice and Folly painted in all their Deformity and Horror. You will ever remember that all the End of study is to make you a good Man and a useful Citizen—This will ever be the Sum total of the Advice of your affectionate Father, John Adams" (Adams 1781).

President John Adams also once famously wrote, "I must study politics and war that my sons may have liberty to study mathematics and philosophy. My sons ought to study mathematics and philosophy, geography, natural history, naval architecture, navigation, commerce, and agriculture, in order to give their children a right to study painting, poetry, music, architecture, statuary, tapestry, and porcelain" (Adams 1780). This is what our founders hoped for us; this is what they sacrificed for us. They expected us to be educated in the classical sense, to be informed, and to continually strive to be a virtuous people. As Professor Steve Turley notes, the word education, translated from Latin, means "to lead out." Where are we being led to? The answer is simple, yet complex ... to freedom (Turley 2022)!

As noted by E.J. Hutchinson, in today's society, "All of these assertions [on virtuous education], however, require thought to unpack, and thinking with the great minds of the past is one way to do this. *This is so, not because they give us the answers, but because they give us the questions and help us as we search for the answers. These answers will not be found on cable news.* Cable news exists to keep us shouting at each other long enough to become fatigued so that we will then carry on our entertainment by other means. *The search described above requires calm and repose; it requires the opposite of what advertising wants to sell you. It requires meditation on thinkers like Aristotle, Cicero, and many others. Its end is to help you to be a good citizen. Its end is to help you be a good neighbor. This is what liberal education, when it is functioning as it should, is for"* (Hutchinson 2018).

Young men and women readers, to learn of great minds, you are encouraged to learn from the best books. Learn your great American history, its flaws, and its amazing triumphs. Read books of noble works from all across the globe. Read books that celebrate beauty. Read books about men and women of good character. Read books on human nature, psychology, the tragedy of war, and the beauty of love. Read the noble stories of good and evil struggles. Educate yourselves in beauty and in truth. Be intelligent, be mentally engaged, be informed, and organize bodies of learning with fellow patriots and neighbors (aka book clubs). Then, watch the tapestry of history unfold before your eyes and understand the loveliness of mathematics and science as well as religion and tradition. For, intelligence is a divine gift and "Freedom is made safe through Character and Learning" ("Traditions" 2022).

Parents, actively participate in your children's education. The current education system fails to teach critical thinking but rather indoctrinates. Sadly, it is a socialistic structure by design. Therefore, consider alternatives to public education. There is an explosion of educational opportunities in classically trained religious schools and homeschooling. We clearly see the evidence that public education at all levels, from elementary school to college, is failing our children. It is time to end support for these failed public institutions. One has to ask, what is the purpose of the Department of Education? What is the purpose of the National Educational Association union when they do not educate and openly support indoctrination? It is time for a movement to disassemble and permanently dismantle these entities as statistics alone demonstrate children are far behind their counterpart's globally; they are failing to educate.

We cannot live without truth. We cannot live without understanding the wisdom and virtues brought about by faith, traditions, and family throughout the ages. Where do we get these truths? We get them, in part, from books through which stories are conveyed on time-honored and tested values, learned and passed down from the ancients to the present. We, as a nation and as a people, cannot live without knowledge that builds, compassionately supports, and promotes the safety and happiness that lies in liberty. Indeed, we cannot live without understanding who we are. To be free, we, too, cannot live without books.

Figure 10. Books donated by Jefferson to the Library of Congress (Purchased Alamy.com 23 Sept. 2022)

Figure 11. "Reading maketh a full man; Conference a ready man; and Writing an exact man." Sir Francis Bacon. Photo taken at Library of Congress, Feb. 2020 by Author

Figure 12. "Wisdom is the principal thing. Therefore, get wisdom and with all thy getting, get understanding." KJV Bible, Proverbs 4:7. Photo taken at Library of Congress, Feb. 2020 by Author

Figure 13. "The foundation of every state is the education of its youth." Diogenes of Sinop, ancient Greek philosopher. Photo taken at Library of Congress, Feb. 2020 by Author

Wisdom of Our Fathers

Support the U.S Constitution, and Learn Accurate
U.S. History

(Honor the Founders & U.S. Constitution)

"We don't need any more statues of dead white men!" yelled the female student at a prominent university event. She emotionally argued about equal rights to protest the university's growth plan. It was the late 1990s, and her point puzzled the listener. The first thought that came to the young man's mind regarding the student's disrespectful and disdainful comment was, "If it weren't for these men, you wouldn't have the right to say silly things like, 'We don't need any more statues of dead white men!'" For you see, many of the "dead white men" may have been young, but their wisdom extended far beyond their mortal years. This unique cast of revolutionary men had a well-informed understanding of the nature of man, including his benevolence, cruelty, and insatiable appetite for power.

How then was the new American government to be formed, they pondered and debated? Fortunately, the wisdom and lessons of the ages were no mystery to the founders, as we shall see in this next story.

At the conclusion of the Constitutional Convention, a very elderly gentleman with the most gravitas, life experience, and greatest accomplishments—a man who embodied the meaning of the United States of America—arose to speak to urge the delegates to sign the Constitution.

✳✳✳

The 81-year-old geriatric could hardly walk anymore; even rising for this momentous occasion elicited great pain. He had poor health and was certainly overweight, even obese. He suffered from gout, a painful build-up of uric acid in his feet, for years. His spectacles betrayed his failing eyesight. He had suffered from obvious skin ailments over the years, too, which scarred his old face. Yet, this man of prominence, intellect, and practical experience proceeded with a speech. That speech resonated with, recognized, and embodied the struggle of the 55 delegates of the Constitutional Convention that just concluded, with a result they felt was nothing short of a miracle.

Addressing the Constitutional Convention's president, General George Washington, Dr. Benjamin Franklin spoke these powerful, wise words to the delegates:

> I confess that I do not entirely approve of
> this Constitution at present, but Sir, I am not
> sure I shall never approve it: For having lived
> long, I have experienced many Instances of
> being oblig'd, by better Information or fuller

Consideration, to change Opinions even on important Subjects, which I once thought right, *but found to be otherwise.* It is therefore that the older I grow the more apt I am to doubt my own Judgment and to pay more Respect to the Judgment of others ...

In these Sentiments, Sir, I agree to this Constitution, with all its Faults, if they are such: because I think a General Government necessary for us, and there is no Form of Government but what may be a Blessing to the People if well administred; and I believe farther that this is likely to be well administred for a Course of Years, *and can only end in Despotism as other Forms have done before it, when the People shall become so corrupted as to need Despotic Government, being incapable of any other.*

I doubt too whether any other Convention we can obtain, may be able to make a better Constitution: *For when you assemble a Number of Men to have the Advantage of their joint Wisdom, you inevitably assemble with those Men all their Prejudices, their Passions, their Errors of Opinion, their local Interests, and their selfish Views. From such an Assembly can a perfect Production be expected? It therefore astonishes me, Sir, to find this System approaching so near to Perfection as it does; and I think it will astonish our Enemies, who are waiting with Confidence to hear that our Councils are confounded, like those of the Builders of Babel, and that our States are on the Point of Separation, only to meet hereafter for the Purpose of cutting one another's Throats. Thus I consent, Sir, to this Constitution because I expect no better, and because I am not sure that it is not the best.*

The Opinions I have had of its Errors, I sacrifice to the Public Good. I have never whisper'd a Syllable of them abroad. Within these Walls they were born, & here they shall die. If every one of us in returning to our Constituents were to report the Objections he has had to it, and endeavour to gain Partizans in support of them, we might prevent its being generally received, and thereby lose all the salutary Effects & great Advantages resulting naturally in our favour among foreign Nations, as well as among ourselves, from our real or apparent Unanimity. *Much of the Strength and Efficiency of any Government, in procuring & securing Happiness to the People depends on Opinion, on the general Opinion of the Goodness of that Government as well as of the Wisdom & Integrity of its Governors. I hope therefore that for our own Sakes, as a Part of the People, and for the Sake of our Posterity, we shall act heartily & unanimously in recommending this Constitution, wherever our Influence may extend, and turn our future Thoughts and Endeavours to the Means of having it well administred.*

On the whole, Sir, I cannot help expressing a Wish, that every Member of the Convention, who may still have Objections to it, would with me on this Occasion doubt a little of his own Infallibility, and to make manifest our Unanimity, put his Name to this Instrument (Mount 2022).

The 55 members of the Constitutional Convention held a wide range of views as they struggled to devise a model of governance. The Articles of Confederation, the current system of government, clearly demonstrated its weak, ineffective, and failing influence as the states failed to function in a "united" fashion, to the glee of the fledging nation's enemies. This reality gave credence to those who wanted a strong central government, like Alexander Hamilton of New York and James

Madison of Virginia. Yet others were extremely distrustful of a strong central government. For example, Elbridge Gerry of Boston, Massachusetts, keenly observed and certainly lived the tyranny brought on by British military and civilian governors in the late 1760s to 1775, leading up to the first shots of the Revolutionary War. While acknowledging the flaws of the Articles of Confederation, this group believed the government's role should primarily be one focused on territorial defense and regulating foreign trade and affairs. But a third cadre of delegates, including George Mason, John Dickinson, Oliver Ellsworth, and John Rutledge, believed in a shared power structure between the Federal Government and the states.

Great notables who influenced the Convention included General George Washington, the Convention's president, and the aforementioned Dr. Benjamin Franklin, as senior statesmen. Both brought an important moderating spirit and credibility to the proceedings.

Those not in attendance but who still had a powerful influence included Thomas Jefferson (performing duties as U.S. Ambassador to France), John Adams (performing duties as U.S. Ambassador to Great Britain), and John's cousin Samuel Adams. Samuel Adams adamantly denounced the idea of a central governmental power as evil. He exercised his powerful voice in the anti-federalist movement, becoming an outspoken proponent of the later adopted Bill of Rights—the first 10 Amendments to the U.S. Constitution.

Patriots, a time for reflection and action.

The delegates were keen students of political and military history, and they were also practical and wise. History was their teacher; philosophy and the benefits of the enlightenment era were their guides. Classically educated in virtue and timeless principles, they studied (to a great extent) the triumphs and trials of Kings and the rise and fall of empires like Jerusalem, Rome, Athens, and other great, terrible, noble, and ignoble empires and their forms of government. They were very well versed in the successes and failures of early republics like Rome and Grecian democracies like ancient Athens. They were further well informed of the British common law, the Magna Carta, and the constitutional system. Moreover, they understood—in very real terms through experience— tyranny, and they equally eschewed and abhorred anarchy. Both extremes never supported individual rights or liberty. The government must ensure as best as possible to prevent either of these extremes from flourishing for overall safety and happiness. The Delegates concluded that a Constitutional form of government with appropriate checks and balances was absolutely necessary for the new nation.

In contrast to the critical arguments made by modern-day academics with master's and doctoral degrees from expensive propaganda diploma mills, the delegates weren't all aristocratic men eager to r e establish an elitist European society. Today's devious ivory-towered intelligentsia and technocrats thumb their noses at the American middle class and sully the U.S. Constitution and the concept of liberty as they pontificate and lecture on how racist, elitist, and outdated the U.S. Constitution is. Their lines of reasoning are foolish at best, and they are malignantly destructive to the freedom and liberty of all mankind, at worst.

Amongst the 55 delegates, 31 attended college. Within the group of classically, college-educated delegates were professors, grammar school teachers or tutors, a college president, lawyers, judges, a minister, and physicians. However, this does not mean the remaining 24 non-college delegates were uneducated fools. Most of these men had humble beginnings, but through their own initiative, abilities, and talents, in the new, untamed land of America, they became prosperous ("Delegates" 2020). These men truly understood and lived the challenges their peer citizens confronted on a daily basis. These delegates were entrepreneurs: businessmen, tradesmen, merchants, farmers, planters, and land speculators. They were what we would deem today as the middle class or perhaps the upper middle class. In fact, many wore multiple hats in these professions or operated diverse businesses. They were not men of leisure or nobility, the equivalent today of trust fund babies; they were workers with talent and ambition.

For example, Dr. Benjamin Franklin did not go to college and only had two years of formal education as a boy. His early life saw him as an indentured servant (a form of slavery requiring years of obedient servitude to acquire a skill) before he escaped to Philadelphia with only a few shillings in his pocket. Yet Dr. Franklin's amazing talents, hard work, literary acumen, community accomplishments, multiple inventions, and scientific discoveries—not to mention his outstanding accomplishments as a diplomat to France and of the pre-war colonial Britain— earned him great accolades from the scientific and philosophical academic heavyweights of his day, to which he earned a doctoral degree.

General George Washington, a "planter" or farmer, did not go to formal college either, but he received an Honorary Doctorate from Harvard in 1776 after he became the Continental Army's general. Washington's library is said to have contained over 1,200 volumes (Pokorski 2022), while Franklin's is said to have contained over 4,000 (Wolf and Hayes 2006). Both men were well-read. Who can doubt their important intellectual contribution to their nation?

Former Brigham Young University Professors Legrand L. Baker and Frank Fox aptly noted:

> In 1740, a mere generation before the Revolution, the intellectual life of America was dominated by clergymen; by 1840, a generation or so after the Revolution, it would be dominated by scientists and inventors. Only for the brief span of a single lifetime would America's statesmen and her brightest thinkers be the same men … They had at their fingertips the best wisdom of their age, for they were in constant touch with the exciting minds of the Enlightenment:

Rousseau, Montesquieu, Voltaire, Hume, Pope, Mandeville, Locke, and Adam Smith … Their study and their experience combined to qualify them for their role in the Convention by preparing them to test their theories against the whole history of mankind's struggle for freedom (Fox and Baker 1976).

But most importantly, they were qualified leaders and citizens, not merely representing their constituents. They led their communities with dignity from the front. They were not spineless career politicians whose positions changed based on the passion of the crowd. They were reasoned and resolute.

The founders were wise leaders in part because they were experienced men who not only reasoned with intellect, but also took action. They did not eschew performing manual labor or aggressively taking practical measures to solve problems. They did not need to ask permission from a faraway body of bureaucrats. They simply acted. These traits were a necessary hallmark of survival since the early days of the Mayflower pilgrims only a little over one and a half centuries before. Further, these men demonstrated resolve through trials and triumphs through real-life, arduous experiences. They exhibited courageous leadership in facing down the world's largest empire and successfully navigating a war. They shared experiences of actual struggles with their communities and neighbors to earn livings for themselves and their families. They worked with their own hands, applied business skills and manual labor, practiced faith, became informed of legal acumen, and demonstrated enlightened learning.

Combined, their aggressive efforts in support of liberty made them resolute, intelligent, and hardy souls. This select band of brothers was uniquely equipped to grapple with the enormous task of founding a new and radically revolutionary form of government. Liberty and individual rights were key cornerstones of this new way of thought at a very unique time in history. And they were determined to build a government based on "negative liberties" to protect their rights as citizens and to promote ingenuity and individual industry for the greatest good of the communities.

"They created a government so well balanced that it prevented any one of its social or geographical factions from getting dominance over the other, a government so strong that it could protect the individual rights of all its citizens and yet so weak that it could not invade their private lives or infringe upon the exercise of their free agency" (Fox and Baker 1976).

Thomas Jefferson proclaimed, "We have spent the prime of our lives in procuring [for the youth of America] the blessing of liberty. Let them spend their lives in showing that it [freedom] is the great parent of science and of virtue; and that a nation will be great in both, always in proportion as it is free" (Jefferson 1789).

CONVENTION AT PHILADELPHIA, 1787.

Figure 14. Signing of the U.S. Constitution, 1787.

(Purchased Alamy.com 23 Sept. 2022)

They Go Where Others Flee & Inspire Charity

Support the Military, Local Law Enforcement, & First Responders

*I*t takes a special kind of person to cultivate the bravery necessary to face danger, with the thoughts they may never come out of hell alive. Yet, so many of these brave souls in the nation, our members of the military, local law enforcement, and first responders, do just that—every single day. Their wages are nothing special. They do not eat steak and lobster for dinner every night. Oftentimes, they are simple, decent folks, trying their best to do their duty and love and raise their families. They are bashful when they are honored or thanked; most do not seek the limelight. And yet, in the glowing fires of the netherworld, they run suppressing fears, breathing hard, with chests pounding and highly focused energies because they understand one important fact —if they do not do this calling, who will? They do so, not because they worry about what others expect of them, they do so because they expect it of themselves. In return, they inspire love, respect, and kindness in the charity they give to great measure beyond themselves.

On a beautiful Tuesday morning, Frank Siller's house bombilated with activity as his entire family arrived for a day of activities together. Frank's wife and sisters prepared a hearty breakfast, the television was on, and talk and laughter filled the house with a loving familial warmth. Suddenly, shocking images of the World Trade Center engulfed in flames appeared on the television screen. All went silent.

Stephen's Story

Stephen Siller was born in NYC in 1967, the youngest of seven children. Tragedy touched Stephen's life at a tender age—his mother died when he was eight years old. Within a year of his mother's passing, his father also died, leaving Stephen an orphan by the age of nine. He grew up in the care of his older brother Frank and other relatives. By all accounts, Stephen was a kind and caring individual. His experience with tragedy and loss left him with a desire to help others. His compassion for those in danger or in need is what led him to pursue a career with New York City's Fire Department, FDNY. Athletic, he took to the grueling physical demands of firefighting with relative ease. He married Sally, literally, the girl next door. Together they had five children and lived in Staten Island, New York.

Stephen arrived at Squad 1 firehouse in Brooklyn, where he was stationed. The overnight watch was uneventful, and as his shift ended,

Stephen stowed his gear in his locker, briefed the relieving shift, said goodbye to his friends, got in his truck, and headed for home. As he made his way through the hectic Brooklyn morning rush hour towards the Staten Island ferry, Stephen made a phone call to his wife, Sally, letting her know that he was on his way home, and to tell his brothers he would meet with them later. Stephen's brothers were just then gathering at Frank's house, waiting for Stephen to arrive. They planned to play a round of golf when Stephen's shift ended.

At 8:46 a.m. on the morning of 11 September, American Airlines flight 11 crashed into the North Tower of the World Trade Center in lower Manhattan. The upper floors of the tower were immediately engulfed in flames. Within minutes, Stephen's scanner squawked to life. He quickly turned his truck around and headed back to the firehouse. He arrived only to discover that Squad 1 had already deployed to lower Manhattan. Stephen grabbed his 60 pounds of fire gear, threw it in his truck, and headed for the Brooklyn Battery Tunnel, which led to lower Manhattan. When he arrived, security had already blocked the entrance to the tunnel. Undeterred, Stephen parked his truck, donned his gear, and ran three miles through the tunnel and all the way to the WTC. At 9:03 a.m., United Airlines flight 175 crashed into the South Tower, creating a deadly inferno. Below, Squad 1 deployed and began rescue operations inside the tower. Stephen likely met up with his squad, and within minutes, he made his way up dozens of flights of stairs to rescue survivors. At 9:59 a.m., the South Tower collapsed, heaving a black belly of smoke and dust for blocks in every direction. Stephen Siller, Squad 1, and an untold number of others were all dead. (Stephen Siller 2022).

Frank's Story

Like every American on that beautiful September morning, Frank, his wife, and his brothers and sisters were fixated on the horrifying images flashing across the TV screen. Minutes after the first crash, Frank received a phone call from Stephen saying not to wait for him, that he would catch up with his brothers later. At around noon, Frank received a call from a friend of Stephen's, a fireman stationed with a different squad. He told Frank that Stephen was among the missing. Not comprehending, Frank replied that he hadn't heard from Stephen but that he was sure that he would soon. The caller told Frank that the situation was really bad. Frank replied that he thought Stephen would call soon. The caller replied to Frank, "Frank! You're not hearing me. Stephen's not coming home. He's gone." Frank later recalled that as the conversation was on speaker phone, his brothers and sisters overheard. He said that his sister let out a wail of grief that haunts him to this day (Frank Siller 2022).

Patriots, a time for reflection and action.

This powerful story reflects who we truly are as Americans and how special and important our first responders, local law enforcement, and military personnel are to this nation.

The phrase, "Greater love hath no man than this, that a man lay down his life for his friends," rings a distinct clarion proclamation of an important eternal truth (John 15:13 [KJV]). The eternal truth is that as we give our lives in service, giving no thought to our own with diligence and purity, we become changed creatures. Our recognition of the eternal soul, worth, and importance of others propels the best of humanity and inspires the same in others. In effect, an important and eternal ripple effect sends its powerful spiritual and temporal waves to brighten and highlight the meaning of love, truth, beauty, and charity.

Stephen Siller exemplified and personified this truth and demonstrated the goodness and determination we inherited from our ancestors in the most remarkable of ways. To run three miles into hell wearing firefighting gear attests to his selfless determination and grit to aid his fellow men and women from the extraordinary disaster before him, is a remarkable feat.

But even more amazing, Stephen's sacrifice initiated an eternal ripple effect, which inspired his brother, Frank. A few days after that black day, Frank spoke with Stephen's wife, Sally. He told her that he wanted to do something to honor Stephen and the sacrifice that so many made on that day. He developed the idea of starting a foundation that would honor and memorialize first responders' sacrifices, but most importantly, would help their families, especially the children who had lost fathers and mothers. The Tunnel to Towers Foundation was born. Every year, the foundation sponsors a

5K race through the Brooklyn Battery Tunnel. In 2021, more than 40,000 people participated in the race. The foundation's *raison d'etre* is to help the families of first responders. This goal is accomplished by paying off the mortgages of first responders killed in the line of duty.

Not long after Tunnel to Towers Foundation comenced, Frank realized that the War on Terror, unleashed after 9/11, was producing large numbers of grievously wounded service men and women. The foundation's mission expanded to help them as well. For those servicemen and women who have lost arms and legs, the foundation builds smart houses to accommodate the needs of wheelchair-bound veterans. Frank Siller's desire to honor his brother's courage and sacrifice has profoundly touched the hearts and lives of hundreds of grief-stricken families. In so doing, Tunnel to Towers has taken a tragic negative and turned it into an enduring positive. Further, think of the inspiration and lesson taught to the children Stephen Siller left behind.

Charity is a word derived from the Latin, *caritas, caritatem*, meaning "love." It carries the connotation of a pure form. Often, it is a translation of the Greek *agape*, which carries the same meaning and connotation. Charity is also synonymous with the Latin word *dilectio*, the noun form of the verb *diligere*, meaning "to esteem highly, to love," and which also has the same root for the word *diligence* or "constant and earnest effort to accomplish what is undertaken; constancy in the performance of duty or the conduct of business; persistent exertion of body or mind; industry; assiduity"

(Online Etymology Dictionary 2022). In Old English, it can be roughly translated to the pure love of Christ or Christian love.

What do you and your family do to show charity? Certainly, supporting a worthy cause by donating money is helpful and much appreciated. But beyond dropping a few bills into a coffer, pot, or mailing envelope, what do you do to show diligence to a cause? Families or individuals who have exercised charity have performed actions such as working in soup kitchens, visiting the widowed, helping the elderly by providing meals or caring for their lawns, and helping clean up after a natural disaster. These actions of *agape, dilectio,* have a much more meaningful and deep impact on young souls than simply dropping change into a Salvation Army container at Christmas time. It reminds us of who we are and the role we play in helping each other in this tough life. It gives us a chance to reflect and be grateful for what we have. And in doing so, it builds good character, which can have a profound impact for generations.

Figure 15. Firefighters on 9/11/2001 in NYC watching WTC towers burn (Purchased Alamy.com 23 Sept. 2022)

Socialist Experiment Nightmare

Support Local Business & Capitalism to Build Community & Reject Socialism

*M*any think that socialism and commune experiments started in Europe and Russia with the advent of Karl Marx's literary works, *The Communist Manifesto* and *Das Kapital*. However, would it surprise you to learn one of the earliest experiments in socialism began in the state of Indiana, much earlier than Marx's works of political theory? Indeed, New Harmony, Indiana, became an experiment founded and led by a prosperous industrialist. Like all socialist dreams, they start with sincere, good intentions to improve the plight of the poor and downtrodden. Inevitably, these dreams—not based on the realities of human nature and desire—become nightmares for those who soon learn the system imposes server limitations on their ability to thrive and exercise personal liberty. It did not take long for the New Harmony dream to become a nightmare. Socialism, in any form, fails, and at many layers, and must be contained and removed from American society. This is because socialism only does one thing well—socialism destroys what is good in the name of "equity" and "fairness," which is fundamentally a lie.

***

A young Welsh-born man walked the dirty streets of the industrial area in Scotland. Thick, black smoke from coal and wood mixed in the industrial air, sticking onto the buildings and giving the structures a permanent gritty and grimy look. The grime filled nostrils and lungs with the toxic particulates, causing ailments of all kinds to the city's inhabitants, as evidenced by the coughing, almost choking noises that frequently sounded from the people. Worse, though, was what he witnessed as he observed the working poor, especially the children. A stench emitted from the scrawny, sickly, starved folks, working themselves to the bones in various factories, blended into the dismal, grey scene. "There has to be a better, more moral way of ensuring the people, and especially the children, are taken care of. 'I shall set out to improve their plight and demonstrate it can be done profitably,'" Robert Owen thought to himself.

Robert Owen hailed from Newtown, Montgomeryshire, Wales. He trained as a draper and became an apprentice at the age of 10. After his apprenticeship, he found employment and training throughout his life until he finally became partner in a cotton mill at the age of 20. "[His] apprenticeship and connection with factory management … [threw him] into daily contact with the toiling classes which was largely to influence his conduct as an employer" (Lockwood 1905, 47). Owen came of age at the advent of the Industrial Revolution.

The Industrial Revolution took place from the late 1700s to the early 1900s, sweeping over Britain and North America before spreading globally. The shift from traditional, manual manufacturing and farming practices to machine-operated production meant jobs for the working class became scarcer while output increased, giving more wealth, control, and power *to factory owners and employers*. This resulted in employers paying their employees less while neglecting safe working conditions because there were so few jobs available and so many in need of employment. The Industrial Revolution also meant that smaller proprietors and family businesses were unable to compete because they could not afford the new machinery and could not keep up with production levels. Many of these smaller businesses failed, resulting in a deterioration of the relationship between employee and employer (Lockwood 1905, 44).

The Industrial Revolution resulted in "[t]he English laboring classes, but a generation before happy, independent, and respected, [becoming], in effect, slaves to their grasping employers." This environment initiated the rise of a "school of philosophers who advocated a reorganized society based upon higher conceptions of public duty" (Lockwood 1905, 45). Recognition of the employers' moral and ethical duty to provide for their employees to the best of their ability was beginning to take hold as societal troubles began to plague England. After the riots of 1811, Robert Owen, who was one of the social philosophers advocating these changes, and his followers began to be taken seriously (Lockwood 1905, 53). Historians note, "[t]he condition of the children employed in factories especially appealed to him. Denied a knowledge of even the elements of education, separated from all the influences of home which are so important a determinant of character, children of honest parents were forced to work side by side with those brought from the workhouses to labor at starvation wages. These children were habitually flogged and debarred from moral and religious instruction" (Lockwood 1905, 48).

On January 1, 1800, Robert Owen took ownership of his father-in-law's spinning mills in New Lanark, Scotland. Appalled by the awful working conditions of the working poor at the early advent of the Industrial Revolution, Owen actively thought about and implemented policies that helped his employees and their families obtain a higher quality of life and education for their children while making a profit. Owen's compassion and tireless efforts certainly made him a popular employer and a known celebrity of sorts in England. Finding initial success, he effectively campaigned throughout England in support of policies and laws that were bent toward his new societal ideas. However, his vocal contempt for religion made him an unpopular public figure among potential supporters and investors in his theories.

Determined to prove his theories of societal accord, Owen purchased 30,000 acres in the new country in the spring of 1825 with the goal of building up a commune in

New Harmony, Indiana. Dignitaries and politicians came to witness this endeavor, with particular interest piqued by the political classes in America and Europe. Initially, many were optimistic and hopeful about New Harmony's success. Using the U.S. Constitution as a prop to bolster his theories, Owen "declared the United States Constitution [marked] the greatest progress of mankind so far made in the direction of liberty" (Lockwood 1905, 66).

Robert Owen enticed many men of renowned intellect to come and live in New Harmony. Owen's premier project included the establishment of an education system for all the children in the community. To that end, Owen enlisted William Maclure, a wealthy scientist who combined ideas on education and political economy (also known as the "Father of American Geology"), to help and give gravitas to the education endeavor. Thomas Say, "the Father of American Zoology," was brought to New Harmony by Mr. Maclure, along with other scientists and educators who were highly accomplished. Another New Harmony notable, Alexander Campbell ("the focus of enlightened atheism"), joined. Owen and his intellectual cabal intended to "make New Harmony the center of American education through the Pestalozzian system of instruction" (Lockwood 1905, 75).

The Pestalozzi method focused on whole-person development, not just giving students facts to memorize to help establish a "New Moral World." According to Owens, "The New Moral World is an organization to rationally educate and employ all, through a new organization of society which will give a new existence to man by surrounding him with superior circumstances only" (Lockwood 1905, 59). In sum, these combined philosophies were intended to cut familial bonds, private property, and religion from the lives of the people. Further, they cut virtuous principles that bound a people to their community. The Founding Fathers would be appalled at such ideas.

Robert Owen's extreme aversion to religion, familial bonds, and private property in the name of "equality" for all, with a promise of a free-thinking society, attracted many intellectual elites. New Harmony became the destination for many "enlightened and progressive people from all over the United States and northern Europe" (Lockwood 1905, 82). Owen proclaimed, "Rational government will attend solely to the happiness of the governed. There must be liberty and conscience and speech. Private property must be abandoned … There should be no rewards or punishments except those awarded by nature" (Lockwood 1905, 66). He convinced himself that organized religion and its view of human nature was foolish. Owen fervently advocated that given the right environment and the right education, people would not behave in selfish, individualistic ways.

On the 50th Anniversary of the signing of the Declaration of Independence, Owen openly stated, "I now declare to you and to the world that man up to this hour has been in all parts of the earth a slave to a trinity of the most monstrous evils that could be combined to inflict mental and physical evil upon the whole race. I *refer to private or individual property, absurd and irrational systems of religion, and marriage founded upon individual property* ... Our principles will spread from community to community, from State to State, from continent to continent, until this system and these principles shall overshadow the whole earth, shedding fragrance and abundance, intelligence and happiness upon all the sons of men" (Lockwood 1905, 146).

However, as more people joined New Harmony to experience this exciting social experiment, cracks in this society began to show. Owen initially established separate communities in an attempt to foster a perfect, harmonious solution to various problems. But as problems arose, Owen decided he needed to superintend with a heavier hand and a streamlined central governance. On September 17, 1826, Robert Owen submitted a proposal to abolish all existing communities and form a new general community called The New Harmony Community Number 1. "The government of this community ... should be invested in [Mr. Owen] and four directors to be appointed by him ... The existing communities did not at once concur to this plan. The members of the educational society denounced it as despotism ... The educational society opposed this plan so vigorously that its supplies were cut off for a few days" (Lockwood 1905, 151). But problems persisted, and socialism's cancerous effects spread.

"The people of the town continued strangers to each other, in spite of all their meetings, their balls, their frequent occasions of congregating in the hall, and all their pretense of cooperation" (Lockwood 1905, 148).

"The mechanics became confused in the intricate machinery created by their constitution, and relieved themselves by abolishing their numerous offices, and creating in their stead a trinity of dictators, which they blasphemously called God the Father, God the Son, and God the Holy Ghost ... The gardens and fields were almost entirely neglected ... A pilfering spirit ... pervaded the place ... The children ... ran morally mad ... [F]rom neglect of the principles of the system, some very well-meaning individuals are committing mistakes which deprive them of the enjoyment of a happy state of mind" (Lockwood 1905, 149–50).

"Money was in higher repute than in any other town and became almost an object of worship. The sexes fought like cats and dogs about individual marriages; there was no politeness between the single persons of the two sexes, but a dark, sullen, cold, suspicious temper, and a most intolerable, miserly allusion to individual property as the standard of worth ... Everyone was for himself, as the saying is" (Lockwood 1905, 157).

"Many [families], after their arrival, have been deprived of more or less of their property, and a general system of trading speculation exists among them, each one trying to get the best of the other. Confidence cannot, therefore, exist among them, and there is an unreasonable spirit of suspicion prevalent. *Inexperience in community enterprises is another great obstacle, and education alone can overcome these difficulties*" (Lockwood 1905, 153–54).

After only two years, it became apparent that even New Harmony's new education was not enough to help the people living in New Harmony overcome their tendency towards individualism. The industrious members left. Robert Owen returned to New Harmony in 1828 after an extended trip to Europe. On his return, he admitted the social experiment failed. Robert Owen went back to Scotland, leaving what was left of the New Harmony estate to his four sons. "One by one these societies became disorganized by dissension, and when Robert Owen returned to New Harmony, on April 1, 1828, his optimism failed in the face of complete collapse of the 'social system' …" (Lockwood 1905, 174).

Robert Owen blamed the poor quality of the people of New Harmony. Owen's son, New Harmony resident and two-term Congressman Robert Dale Owen, disagreed with his father, writing, "All cooperative schemes which provide equal remuneration to the skilled and industrious and the ignorant and idle must work their own downfall. For by this unjust plan, they must of necessity eliminate the valuable members and retain only the improvident, unskilled, and vicious" (Lockwood 1905, 222). Further, the New Harmony intelligencia failed to recognize an important point—to succeed, one needs workers, not mere thinkers. Central planners think command and control produce success while they dine and wine off the backs of the laborer. In their hubris, they fail to see the variables are too many to control. Attempts to control only make matters worse, not better.

Patriots, a time for reflection and action.

Critics of the U.S. Constitution and the foundational principles, values, and virtues that formed the United States advocate that the New Harmony utopian ideals are exactly what the country and the world need. Many of the "elite" believe in the use of force to achieve ends, much like the New Harmony leadership. For example, using environmentalism and sustainability as an excuse, a Blackrock billionaire oligarch recently quipped, "Behaviors are going to have to change, and this is one thing we are asking companies, you have to force behaviors and … we are forcing behaviors" (Mathews 2022). In their minds, the failure of such societies is the fault of the people, not the beloved theory or concept—which ultimately leads to forced compliance. Yet, societies that implement the practices of socialism fail in the end, always. Its decrepit system requires submission and only benefits the iron-fisted "leadership" and business cronies who make money from the scheme. The people become poor; the so-called leaders (or tyrants) become rich.

To illustrate, in Cuba, the late President Fidel Castro's net worth was estimated at $900 million when he died (Marcin 2016). Yet, today the average Cuban makes about $25,000, with the highest workers making $66,000 per year (Rafael 2022). Moreover, to this day, the Cuban people suffer to get basic needs and food. The political undesirables, thousands of them, have been murdered over the years. The Cuban people wallow much like the 1820s New Harmony residents, making the Caribbean Island nation much like the following description of New Harmony, "The gardens were neglected, and though several skilled gardeners lived in the community, much ground lay fallow, which might have made handsome gardens. The people, instead of employing their thoughts to execute their work well, were musing on plans of new arrangements in the system of government of the society." (Lockwood 1905, 140). After all, community members must be occupied with what the government looks like and whatever new edict the government expects to be followed since the regime runs every aspect of their lives. They must do so and submit to the government in order to survive.

As George Orwell (1945) wrote in his best-selling work, *Animal Farm*, "All animals are equal, but some animals are more equal than others." Do we not see it in the language and forceful arguments today? The hysterically vocal part of society use and abuse positions of power to further their socialistic aims. For example, faux tolerance devoid of reason and logic to the catastrophic consequences to children, demands for digital "vaccine" passports to travel and work, forced experimental mandates injected into the body against one's will for community "protection" with threats of job loss or community segregation, and use Environmental Sustainability and Governance (ESG) scores to rank social desirability. Yet, while this vocal, elite minority demand compliance to their will, they will hypocritically flaunt the rules they demand for their own benefits. Liberty is based on the right of self-defense and family defense, yet, the perpetually aggrieved and the intelligencia demand in the name of "safety" the elimination of firearms. Further, the abolition of private property, children miseducated and "owned" by the state, and the pointed attack on faith are openly promoted by the same class. Does this not sound like Owen's prediction?

These highlight the need for a strong and vibrant middle class. *Mesio*, from the Greek word for the middle ones, have been a crucial body of citizens since our founding. Dr. Victor Davis Hanson notes key attributes of the *Mesio* include, "Seats and votes in the assembly, military service in the phalanx, [and] ownership of agrarian land … The independence of the middle class also required that they combine physical labor with mental acuity in making decisions about their livelihoods" (Hanson 2021).

The importance of the middle class cannot be understated. The middle class is the sane citizenry that keep the nation functioning. Their active participation in citizenry and politics protects against the powerful, wealthy elites who use money and position to influence policy for their personal benefit. Simultaneously, the *mesio* protect against excessive requests for public financial support from the indigent in society, particularly those whose choices demand an ever-increasing share of "free services" drawn from the public treasury, with no intention to repay or contribute back to society. The *mesio* are a crucial part of the "checks and balances" the founders envisioned. A virtuous *mesio* is needed to keep the overall nation intact.

In recent years, there has been an all-out assault by both the wealthy and the poor on the *mesio*. Manufacturing moved overseas for profit on slave labor in nations like China and low-cost labor in Mexico. These policies forced the middle class to find employment in cities instead of their local communities to survive or live near poverty conditions in their depressed communities. During the COVID-19 pandemic, public officials threatened small business owners, the middle class, with fines and closures during the pandemic, yet "big box" stores could remain open. Further, these public officials and politicians love to stoke the fires of envy, claiming the middle-class business owners are taking advantage of the poor and becoming "rich" at their expense. Note the parallels to what happened in New Harmony, Indiana.

What can you do?

To counteract this trend, buy American, and buy local whenever you can. Support families by frequenting family businesses or locally owned and locally operated franchises. Support local credit unions and community banks. Frequent local restaurants as opposed to chain eateries. Purchase fruits and vegetables at local farmers' markets. Are these more expensive? Yes, often they are.

However, consider the importance of these vendors and small business owners. They are vital creators and astute entrepreneurs. Strolling down the aisles of these markets, the colorful and creative stalls teem with beautiful, quality artifacts, products, services, and foods. In the event of shortages and supply chain issues (remember 2020–2021?), the *mesio* use the freedom of thought, speech, directed ambition, and talents to create products or services a community wants. These are the folks needed in times of crisis. Their self-reliant natures, resilience, skill, autonomy, and discipline strengthen and bind the community through their service and talents. Contributing your money to them to let them serve you not only supports their endeavors, it strengthens you. It strengthens your community and makes you and your family less dependent on centralized sources who often provide inadequate care or solutions, usually with strings attached or force.

We cannot and should not rely on subpar products from the adversarial People's Republic of China. Contributing to foreign companies makes our nation weaker. Further, we should refrain, as best as possible, from fattening the pockets of technology executives, who have disdain for the *mesio* and its values, who cancel speech and payment processing to comport to their own destructive "community standards." Many of these executives are in league with the unelected, unaccountable world bodies such as the Open Society or World Economic Forum—an unwise and wicked cabal that believes, once again, they can resurrect Robert Owen's grand New Harmony experiment and create a utopia—but this time ruling with technology.

Finally, align with family and businesses that align with the Values We Hold Dear, or, even better, start your own business. The concept of a parallel society (aka a parallel economy or parallel polis) is taking root. There are phone "apps," like PublicSq, and social media companies and the like, that align with your values. The media and technology giants, while outrageously wealthy and suffocatingly stubborn, will eventually fail.

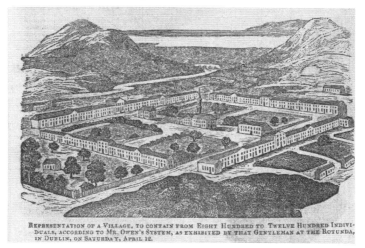

Figure 16. New Harmony, Indiana circa 1820s

(Purchased Alamy.com 23 Sept. 2022)

A Young Lad's Dream

Recognize Every Life Has Value, Reject Racism

"All men are created equal" is a seminal phrase in the Declaration of Independence. In the context of the 1770s, the phrase "all men" referred to "all humanity." America's history with race relations is very complex—at times very inspiring, and at other times very heartbreaking. Like a messy divorce, the evolving and complex issues surrounding racism have left permanent scars on our national psyche, and it has taken a long and painful process to accept reality and move forward to right the wrongs of the past. However, one should ask, what nation has done more to live up to the phrase "e pluribus unum"? While Great Britain led the way in abolishing slavery, America spilt much blood in the U.S. Civil War to end slavery and continued to fight for civil rights.

What nation or people have done more to recognize and correct errors of the past? The beauty of the foundation built and gifted to us by the Founding Fathers and Mothers gave life to this movement. To be sure, the Founding Fathers were men of their time. But let this story of James illustrate that the Founders built a solid infrastructure in our government to enable equality and justice for all very early on. It has taken a lot of soul-searching work to grow and harvest the fruits to form a union where all humanity is recognized as equal. America did so, and despite the cries for "change" by authoritarian forces, America will remain vigilant in supporting life and denouncing racism.

∗∗∗

Dare James ask permission from his employer? What if the lady said no? Would he be humiliated? He agonized over this decision. But the quest for the opportunity to go to school burned in James. Sure, he earned a fair living as a laborer, but he wanted the same opportunities—equal opportunities—as his friends had.

The opportunity to grow, learn, and excel beyond one's own station in life was all he wanted. As a hireling to a prominent family, he worked the rocky New England land to help grow food and take care of the farm. From the rocky soil, he backbreakingly unearthed grey stones and built stone walls to mark the property boundaries, a practice common to many a home in New England. He was popular, made friends easily, and was respected and liked. He attended the local Congregational church, the centerpiece edifice of the community. James' employer liked him too, and James was fond of his employer, though he rarely saw the head of the household. The beautiful and articulate lady ran the key business affairs and did very well. She had been doing this for many years, including during the War for Independence when her beloved husband was away (Adams 1797).

James finally asked his employer. He would like to go to school to learn; may he enroll? He would like to join his friends. Would the lady of the house permit time for him to do so?

The lady of the house readily agreed to the request, providing James receiving approval from the school's headmaster, Mr. Heath. Master Heath heartily accepted James's request. Happily, he got his wish to improve his mind! And what's more, the lady of the house agreed to pay for it!

But not all in the small community thought this was wise. One evening, a neighbor, Mr. Faxon, approached the lady at her residence.

The lady noted, "His errand was to inform me that if James went to school, it would break up the school as the other lads refuse to go!"

"Was James misbehaving?" she asked with surprise in her voice.

"O no, there was no complaint of that kind ..." replied neighbor Faxon, looking down with furrowed brow.

"Did these lads ever object to James playing for them when at a dance?" She inquisitively persisted. "Really? Who is objecting to James's learning to read and write?" the lady continued.

"O, it is not I that object or my boys; it is some others," neighbor Faxon defensively answered.

"It's not your lads, then who's lads?" The lady impatiently questioned, sensing a hidden agenda. "Further, why did they not come themselves? *This Mr. Faxon is attacking the Principle of Liberty and equality upon the only ground upon which it ought to be supported …*"

The lady was measured in her tone and response but internally irate. For, you see, James was a freeman, a black freeman, and according to neighbor Faxon, the other boys did not "choose to go to school with a black boy."

"*An equality of rights, the boy is a freeman as much as any of the young men, and merely because his face is black, is he to be denied instruction? How is he to be qualified to procure a livelihood? Is this the Christian Principle of doing to others as we would have others do to us?*" the lady resolutely challenged neighbor Faxon.

The old neighbor, recognizing his folly in the visit, responded, "You are quite right. I hope you will not take offense."

"None at all, Mr. Faxon, only be so good as to send the young men to me. I think I can convince them that they are wrong. I have not thought it any disgrace to myself to take him into my parlour and teach him both to read & write—tell them, Mr. Faxon, that I hope we shall all go to Heaven together."

Mr. Faxon nervously laughed. Tipping his hat in a gesture to respectfully signal good evening to the revered lady, he departed (Adams 1797).

She deserved respect. She earned that respect after the numerous trials of farm life, raising three children alone during the war, and enduring the years of her husband's absence. That was not all.

The lady, Abigail Adams, was also the first lady of the new nation. Her husband, President John Adams, conducted his duties at the new White House on the Potomac River in Maryland while she took care of the farm in Quincy, Massachusetts.

For modern-day naysayers who claim that all the citizens of this great nation were elitist and racist, this true story demonstrates this was not so. Abigail Adams rightly challenged neighbor Faxon's notion of liberty and was ready to teach James herself. Further, Headmaster Heath would not deny James an education. Two people in the Massachusetts township outside of Boston stood firm and courageously declared that every life had worth.

Patriots, a call for reflection and action.

Remember and teach your posterity how radical of a notion this was. The colonists just freed themselves from an empire that, for centuries, was an elitist, hierarchical based society, one that treated the colonists as second-class subjects whose sole purpose in life was to produce and sell to fill the treasury of the king. Further, societies whose leadership derived from the "divine right of kings" had been around for centuries. The notion that ALL men were created equal and could govern themselves was an experiment; it had never really been done well before.

Even the first draft of the Declaration of Independence, written in Thomas Jefferson's own hand, included the clause denouncing the notion of slavery in support of the idea that all were created equal.

The draft passage reads, "He has waged cruel war against human nature itself, violating its most sacred rights of life and liberty in the persons of a distant people who never offended him, captivating and carrying them into slavery in another hemisphere or to incur miserable death in their transportation thither. This piratical warfare, the opprobrium of infidel powers, is the warfare of the Christian King of Great Britain. Determined to keep open a market where Men should be bought and sold, he has prostituted his negative for suppressing every legislative attempt to prohibit or restrain this execrable commerce. And that this assemblage of horrors might want no fact of distinguished die, he is now exciting those very people to rise in arms among us, and to purchase that liberty of which he has deprived them, by murdering the people on whom he has obtruded them: thus paying off former crimes committed against the Liberties of one people, with crimes which he urges them to commit against the lives of another" (Jefferson 2022).

Sadly, the passage condemning slavery did not make it into the final version of the Declaration of Independence. It was the one passage certain colonies in both the South and North could not support, in part due to the profitability of the slave trade. The Founders decided the issue would have to be reexamined after defeating Great Britain. This is quite strong evidence that the Founding Fathers were on a path to build a nation where eventually, all could be partakers of freedom. Further evidence of this notion is found in President Washington's last Will & Testament, where he required, "Upon the decease ⟨of⟩ my wife, it is my Will & desire th⟨at⟩ all the Slaves which I hold in ⟨my⟩ own right, shall receive their free⟨dom⟩" (Washington 1799).

While it is true remnants of British hierarchy still persisted in the newly formed nation, one must ask, how could it not? For millennia, in all parts of the globe, this was commonplace. Remember, the p e o p l e p l o w e d t h e soil of true freedom in this virgin land. Experiments would come and go. Some would fail; some would succeed. Many recognized in sweeping ways how freedom and the rights of individual citizenship would be very revolutionary for the new nation. As a nation, we fought three wars over this. The War for Independence, the Civil War, and the Civil Rights war. And the better side won. Teach these truths to your children. We are all created equal, endowed by our creator. Let no one *"attack the Principle of Liberty and equality upon the only Ground upon which it ought to be supported"* (Adams 1797).

Figure 17. A young Abigail Adams (Purchased Alamy.com 23 Sept. 2022)

A Hero's Hanging

Embrace Responsibility, Reject Victimhood

*P*atriots of old were undaunted. They took on callings and responsibilities with poise and integrity that most were unwilling to do. When they failed, they did not shamefully cry or claim they were victims of fraud and therefore deserved special consideration and treatment. With dignity, they took ownership of their lives, their actions, and their responsibilities. Mortal lives were oftentimes extinguished to the eternities doing the right thing with dignity; the ultimate sacrifice divined for something greater. This is a story about one such young patriot.

***

In the waning days of the hot, humid summer of 1776, the hint of fall seeped in to cool the coastal air as a young man embarked on the boat. The intellectually sharp but otherwise unremarkable young man had a mission to fulfill, a mission he solely volunteered for when General George Washington himself asked. Born of religious parents and raised in the remote, quaint village of Coventry, Connecticut, the eloquent, admired Yale College-educated teacher ended his profession as a school teacher. He did this to serve in the Connecticut militia and then later in the 19th Regiment of the Continental Army when war with the British broke out in Massachusetts. His intellect and education qualified him to become a commissioned officer, a Captain in the Regiment. As the ferry crewed by patriots hurriedly departed from Norwalk, Connecticut, to cross the blue-grey, choppy waters of Long Island Sound, Captain Nathan Hale reviewed the mission in his head as he breathed in the salty air. General Washington needed to know the location of British Forces and, more importantly, where they were planning the assault on New York City. Officially, the colonial captain disguised himself as a school teacher looking for work. Unofficially, he was a spy.

Friend and foe alike despised spies in colonial times. Spying was a dirty, dishonest, and dishonorable business conducted by scoundrels. Growing up Congregationalist, a Christian offshoot of the Puritan faith, Nathan Hale's parents raised him to be honest, hardworking, ethical, and pious—traits never associated with spies. Further, being caught spying meant certain death. Nonetheless, Hale volunteered when no one else would, despite how woefully equipped in skill and temperament he was for the craft because General Washington and the glorious cause needed him in this urgent hour.

Alas, his mission was overcome by events. The British launched an invasion of New York before Capt. Nathan

Hale could gather the intelligence and send it to General Washington. Hale decided against returning to Connecticut or rejoining his regiment. Instead, he opted to press on in his role as a spy and see if he could be of service and gather intelligence in other ways.

Unfortunately, nearly as soon as he arrived in New York City, a loyalist Tory recognized the young captain and deceived him with patriotic platitudes over ale at a local pub and invited the young man to dinner. After enjoying a delicious meal with this supposed band of patriots, Hale surprisingly learned his new friends were actually foes. These Tories searched Hale's pouch, where his captors found sketches of British fortifications and writings on British troop strength and positions. Hale's captors had all they needed to confirm that Captain Nathan Hale was a rebel spy. Without hesitation, Captain Nathan Hale faced the indignant wrath of Sir General William Howe, Commander of British forces, who ordered Hale's quick execution by hanging.

One of Hale's captors noted how composed the 21-year-old man appeared when discovered. Frederick MacKensie, a British officer, wrote in his diary, "[Captain Nathan Hale] behaved with great composure and resolution, saying he thought it the duty of every good Officer, to obey any orders given him by his Commander-in-Chief; and desired the Spectators to be at all times prepared to meet death in whatever shape it might appear" (Ortner 2001). Another account noted on the morning of his hanging, Hale "bore himself with great dignity, in the consciousness of rectitude and high intentions."

After being solemnly led to the gallows on the morning of September 22, 1776, the officer in charge offered Captain Nathan Hale a chance to say his last words. It is written that his last words were, "I only regret that I have but one life to lose for my country." However, as a man of educated eloquence who excelled in rhetoric, his last words were likely a spirited speech for liberty, with an ending more akin to, "I am so satisfied with the cause in which I have engaged, that my only regret is, that I have not more lives than one to offer in its service" (Morse 1824, 260).

Patriots, a time for reflection and action.

At the time of the signing of the Declaration of Independence, legend purports Benjamin Franklin eloquently responded to John Handcock's statement that we should "hang together" by observing, "We Must All Hang Together, or Most Assuredly, We Will All Hang Separately." Let us take ownership, interlocked together, and not become victims.

At this very hour, nation-state adversaries like the Peoples Republic of China (the Chinese Communist Party) are looking to destroy the United States. Further, non-state actors like the World Economic Forum (WEF) are actively assaulting us to divide patriots and nationalists across the globe. They openly attack customs, cultures, traditions, and natural rights to institute a new framework to make you their personal subjects, serfs, or slaves to their profit and causes, deceptively in the name of "justice." They aim to reawaken the tyrannical grandeur visions of the Roman Caesars, the Czars, the Emperors, and Kings and Queens of old. By compromise ideally, but by force, if necessary, the WEF would like to see the 1,000-year Reich return to achieving its destruction of liberty and human rights. The leader of the deceitful cabal is a grandfatherly looking but sinister Austrian who openly states, "The people assume, we are just going back to the good old world which we had, and everything will be normal again, in how we are used to be normal in the old fashion. This is, let's say, fiction, it will not happen, the cut which we have now, is much too strong in order not to leave traces" (Woke Media 2021, 0:01:09). They have a plan, and that plan only ends in tyranny and bondage, for you. They do so by persuading the masses that their form of uber governance is supreme and even necessary to "save the planet" for the greater good. But the wise intuitively understand, and know through human history, that these proposals are ultimately oppressive and destructive. We have been here before.

Now is the time to become educated and be prepared for the battle for liberty. Take personal responsibility, and be prepared to speak, write, and think with logic and eloquence to combat this battle for control versus freedom. Reject becoming a victim or falling to the woes of victimhood, and take a stand for your family and your freedoms. Let this poem from 1770s colonial America, a poem that likely inspired Capt. Nathan Hale, to help you to take responsibility and not become a mere victim of their tyrannical horrors. Do so with love, wisdom, courage, and dignity, like Captain Nathan Hale did.

"With public Spirit let each Bosom glow
And Love of Liberty direct the blow
Rouse, patriot Heroes and pursue the plan
Teach listless Souls what 'tis to play the man!"
(Fanestil 2021)

Figure 18. Capt. Nathan Hale's hanging Sept. 1776
(Purchased Alamy.com 23 Sept. 2022)

A Woman's Great Legacy

We Believe Men & Women are Equal

(Men & Women Are Equal in Hoisting a Shield to Protect Families & the Nation)

*M*en have long known that true greatness, power, and grace lie with women. Indeed, fights and even wars have started over women. While men have traditionally held the reigns of political, economic, and military power, this does not mean that women are of any less importance. Impressively, as America grew and emerged as a power, so did the recognition of women's equal and rightful status with men. The following story illustrates the emergence of that recognition. The Founding Fathers, thankfully, planted the seeds to enable equal rights to become a reality.

In 1834, the Hudson Bay Company founded a trading post in this western community for wagon trains just north-west of the city. Oregon Trail emigrants passed through, as did gold prospectors looking for fortune and opportunity in the virgin land. "The determined citizens made it their initiative to make the area livable by developing irrigation systems, planting crops, and mapping out a town with shady streets along the river." By 1868, the city had more than 400 permanent structures. In 1887, a new rail line and train station were fully functional. By 1890, Boise, Idaho, was a beautiful, thriving place to live ("Boise Strikes Gold" 2022).

✳✳✳

A beautiful young woman with long brown hair and lovely brown eyes disembarked from the train after her days-long journey from New York City. The talented California native, the first child and eldest daughter of a former governor of Missouri and the current Mayor of Stockton, had completed her first year at The Arts Student League of New York by the time she arrived in the summer of 1890. Emma stepped off onto the new station's platform of the prosperous and small but bustling city in the expanding western territories. Little did she know she would become a legend and a part of history soon after her heeled boots touched the ground.

Emma traveled to Boise to meet a relative and to stay for a short visit on her way home to California. During her visit, she and her relative would "amuse themselves" by sitting in on the very first legislative sessions of the Idaho House and Senate. She practiced her art by drawing the politicians, becoming "well acquainted" with them, their mannerisms, and their individual features.

Then, an unlikely opportunity arose. A committee from Idaho's House and Senate formed to create a state seal. The committeemen announced a contest would be held.

Three men entered the contest with their various drawings. However, these men clearly were not artists. A shy girl, it took some persuading, but several members of the legislature prevailed upon Emma, knowing she had talent, to submit a design. She felt "incapable of the task" but "consented to submit a drawing." The task was rather tricky, for the committee wanted a full-scale size of the seal. "By sharpening the lead pencils to needle points" and diligently researching the unique characteristics of the 43rd State in the Union, Emma set on her task to create the artwork" ("Emma Edwards Green Papers" 2022).

From her research, she knew that mining was an important industry in Idaho, so she "made the figure of the man the most prominent in the design." Further, Emma knew that the leading politicians would eventually give women the right to vote. With that in mind, she drew "the woman, signifying justice, as noted by the scales; liberty, as denoted by the liberty cap on the end of the spear." But the imagery she wanted captured above all was that in "equality with man as denoted by her position at his side, also signifies freedom … *The shield between the man and woman is emblematic of the protection they unite in giving the state*" ("Emma Edwards Green Papers" 2022).

Emma won the Idaho State Seal contest and its $50 prize (about $1,500 in today's currency), becoming the first and only woman to have designed a state seal in this great nation. However, that was not all of Emma's accomplishments.

After she won the contest, Emma actively promoted the state seal of Idaho as a representative to the 1893 world fair in Chicago, a truly global event. Emma also raised money for the creation of the flag of Idaho with the seal she created as the centerpiece of the banner. Idaho's elected officials saw the new state flag off to war with its newly-formed Idaho military regiment to quell and stabilize the newly acquired Philippines in 1899. Those soldiers later returned with a beautified Idaho flag, the seal gorgeously and magnificently embroidered by Filipino nuns on a striking navy-blue background. The stunning work astounded the officials and citizens of Idaho alike. The beautiful display further validated that Idaho's first leaders made the best choice in choosing Emma's art. At a great ceremony to honor the new flag, the Adjunct General and a fellow citizen lauded her accomplishments. Embarrassed, she recalled, "I remember this as one of the most complimentary talks I have ever heard about myself ..." ("Emma Edwards Green Papers" 2022).

Emma decided to remain in Boise, Idaho, for the rest of her days, not returning to school in New York or moving back to California. Instead, she set up a school of arts for children in the community, helping to bring more beauty and culture to the city. She married and helped build a legacy and lasting contribution to Boise and the state of Idaho.

Those seeds flowered throughout the 19th century as the country expanded westward. Note, too, the men of Idaho recognized that Emma had talent they lacked and encouraged her, not patronized but supported and lauded her important part of Idaho's and this nation's history. These powerful Idaho men recognized times were changing, and who better to represent that change in Idaho than Emma Edwards Green? Thanks to women like Emma, and the men of Idaho that encouraged her, women have served honorably at home and abroad in two world wars, earned advanced degrees, serve honorably in the military, are political leaders, and thrive in all parts of society, not just in America, but globally as well ("Emma Edwards Green Papers" 2022).

Patriots, a time for reflection and action.

This story truly represents America. A young lady, shy, demure, but also full of life, contributed greatly to the building of the nation at a time when men controlled all levers of power. Emma persevered despite her lack of confidence and personal misgivings. She directly contributed to a community, bringing art and refinement to the west. She raised a family; her heritage lives on in Idaho.

Today, a very vocal segment of society argues the American foundation and the Constitution need to be destroyed because patriarchal influence during the formation of the Republic oppressed and suppressed women's equal access and opportunities. Some judgingly point to the Declaration of Independence and opine the phrase "all *men* are created equal" as proof of a misogynist, patriarchal founding. In actuality, in the context of the period, "men" meant "humanity" ("Creating" 2022). Further, many mockingly insulted the founders by protesting, "We don't need statues of dead white men!" *However, the Declaration of Independence, Constitution, and the Founding Fathers actually planted the seed to enable all humanity, especially women, to thrive in the new republic.* Further, we see this in the earliest examples of how Presidents George Washington and John Adams openly recognized the great contributions of their respective wives, Martha and Abigale. These women were crucial companions to the creation of the country. James Monroe of Virginia, the father of the United States Constitution, noted, "I take a deep interest, as a parent and a citizen, in the success of female education, and have been delighted whenever I have been, to witness the attention paid to it." (Monroe 1818, 175)

Men and women are created equal. In equal unity, love, and harmony, man and woman unite to give life to and strengthen their families. By strengthening their families, they fortify their communities, their states, and the nation as a whole.

To strengthen the nation, you must strengthen the family. A wonderful work written in 1976 entitled *Declaration of Dependence: Teaching Patriotism in the Home* by Robert K. Thomas and Shirley Wilkes Thomas precisely hits the importance of the familial theme. "The heart of patriotism … lies in attitudes that are rooted in family relationships, for the family unit, in microcosm, undergoes most of the stresses which test the larger societies that make up a nation. The qualities that distinguish patriotism are all of the 'homely' variety: respect, integrity, loyalty, self-sacrifice, consideration, fairness, appreciation, and devotion. No exhortation to respect his country's flag can mean much to the youngster whose casual, permissive upbringing has left him with little respect for anything. And the child who equates freedom with indulgence may never understand the consideration for others that is fundamental to a workable democracy."

In humility, patience, and love, men and women supporting the greatest of callings to build the traditional family are vital. They ensure the equality and rights of the citizenry are maintained and are key to regaining our national strength.

The United States of America is strongest when this notion of familial love, unity, and harmony is supported and fostered by our leaders. Societies that fail always have a common thread—the division and ultimate destruction of the family. In Hungary, Romania, Vietnam, Russia, Poland, Venezuela, China, and Cuba, the division initiated by insidious forces to remove familial traditions and culture only brought ruin, depression, and destruction.

For example, when the Viet Cong took over a Vietnamese village, one of the first acts was to kill the village elders to instill fear and to control the remaining members. In Romania, Poland, and Hungary, communist party leaders took land from middle-class farmers and made family members work as farmers in different fields far from their homes, and terrorized and imprisoned fathers to divide the family. In China, the Chinese Communist Party expected children to denounce their successful parents or be forced into slave labor as tenant farmers or hard laborers.

Sadly, in this very day and age in America, the ideal of familial bonds and the goodness it fosters is under tremendous siege by a tyrannical administrative state, foolish national and local education boards and school "professionals," and a very imprudent political class. Unwise academic intelligencia and politicians alike have opined that we must disabuse the notion that the traditional family unit is good and that parents have ownership of their children. Further, they argue the state is the ultimate abitur and caretaker of children. Today in America, there is a concerted effort to separate families, which is, in effect, an attack on women as well, who typically shoulder a large portion of the burden (whether single or married) of child-rearing. A former cable host and Tulane Professor Melissa Harris-Perry commented recently, "We have never invested as much in public education as we should have because we've *always had kind of a private notion of children. Your kid is yours and totally your responsibility. We haven't had a very collective notion of these are our children ... So part of it is we have to break through our kind of private idea that kids belong to their parents, or kids belong to their families, and recognize that kids belong to whole communities*" ("Perry" 2013).

Disappointingly, many have been infected with this evil, promoting the breaking of the bonds between man and woman, child and parent. In recent history, Adolf Hitler of Nazi Germany, Mao Tse Tung of Communist China, and Joseph Stalin of the United Soviet Socialist Republic all held the same belief that children are the property of the state.

George Orwell's book *Nineteen Eighty-four* (1949) describes this concept as well in his prescient warning as illustrated by Winston Smith's neighbor, Mr. Parsons, a loyal party member whose own children report him to the state on false charges. We are on a path to destruction, and our posterity will live in serfdom—as in times of old—if we do not course correct and recognize the equal power of men and women to build and sustain the fundamental building block of the family.

To combat this, make your homes sanctuaries for beauty, goodness, and truth. Eat together as a family. Abandon negative influences in the home, such as television and social media, that can disrupt and disengage social connections. Raise your children in truth, honor, and love. Teach and lead by example what it means to be men and women of the Republic. Teach them responsibilities, how to handle conflict productively, how to love, how to work and be responsible, how to be supportive, and how to rightly defend themselves and others that need their help. Read and apply concepts taught in our founding documents in the home. Sing songs with patriotic fervor, and explain their importance and history. Be the example that this nation so desperately needs.

For couples: husbands, love, provide for, and be faithful to your wives. Wives, be supportive, honor, and love your husbands. Both, demonstrate that love and support to your children, to your grandchildren, and to your extended families. For the battle of families is not only a battle we must win; it is the ultimate battle we can and will win. As Emma

Edwards Green aptly noted, "[t]*he shield between the man and woman is emblematic of the protection they unite in giving the state"* (Green 2022).

Figure 19. Idaho State Flag (https://www.britannica.com/topic/flag-of-Idaho 24 Jan 2023)

Figure 20. Emma Edwards Green (https://sos.idaho.gov/elect/bluebook/Histseal.htm 24 Jan 2023).

A National Treasure

We Believe Men & Women are Equal

(The Vital Contributions of Dolley Madison to Liberty)

*T*he wives of our first presidents are an inspiration to us all. All were national treasures that deserve our honor and respect. Martha Washington endured much heartache standing by the side of her husband, General George Washington, during the Revolutionary War and then as president. Abigail Adams urged her husband to "remember the ladies" when forming the new nation (Adams 1776). Martha Jefferson stood by Thomas Jefferson's side during the American Revolution before her untimely death. And Dolley Madison, the wife of James Madison, holds a special place in American history for the important actions she took time and again to propel the United States of America forward. Dolley is a national treasure who, through spirited grace, brought dignity and honor to the nation and saved national treasures.

***

"Damn that man!", the first British Ambassador to America, Sir Anthony Merry, thought to himself at the presidential dinner. Elegantly dressed in fine European attire of the day, Sir Anthony Merry silently seethed during the delicious but clearly unconventional state meal. First, President Thomas Jefferson insulted Merry by appearing in a bathrobe and slippers at their first meeting only days earlier. Second, President Jefferson invited the French ambassador to the official dinner held to honor the British ambassador, a serious affront as President Jefferson well knew eating a meal with one's enemy—Britain and France were at war— was considered disgraceful. Third, instead of escorting Mrs. Elizabeth Merry, the ambassador's wife, to the dinner table— as was protocol and good manners—President Jefferson escorted Mrs. Dolley Madison. Dolley quietly protested to Jefferson, saying that he should not be escorting her, adding he should be escorting Mrs. Merry. Jefferson seemed oblivious or did not care about this significant diplomatic *faux pas*. This "absolute Omission of all Distinction in [his] and Mrs. Merry's Favor" infuriated the proper Anthony Merry (Wilson, Pierce, and Robinson 2022). As dinner ended, the wife of the Spanish minister, another dinner guest, whispered into Dolley Madison's ear, "This will be the cause of war" (Allgor 2007, 85).

Dolley Payne was born in a Quaker community in Guilford County, North Carolina, on May 20, 1768. Her parents, John Payne and Mary Coles, both from prominent

Virginia families, were newly arrived in North Carolina. Dolley was the third of eight children born to the Paynes. In 1769, John Payne abruptly moved his family back to Virginia. Then, in 1783, John Payne moved his family to Philadelphia, where he established a business as a starch manufacturer. There he applied for membership in the local Quaker meeting.

Dolley flourished during her formative years in Philadelphia, blossoming into a beautifully striking young woman. She had sparkling blue eyes, black hair, and a flawless complexion. It was said that every day, men would position themselves near the Payne's home to catch a glimpse of her. Moreover, she was gregarious, friendly, and a natural at the social graces. She had many admirers.

In 1789, John Payne's business failed, leaving him with several unpaid debts. At around the same time, Payne was expelled from the local meeting. Historians Carroll Berkin, John Stagg, and Catherine Allgor assert that Payne's business failure was the result of alcoholism and gambling. The family was shunned by the Quaker community. John Payne never recovered, financially or emotionally. He took to his bed and shut the world out until his death in 1792. Mary, his wife, was forced to take in boarders to make ends meet. John Payne's failure and the family's disgrace would have a profound impact on Dolley. She became, as historians describe, like the child of an alcoholic, eager to avoid conflict and always desiring to make things right.

Before his death, John Payne had arranged for Dolley to marry John Todd, a prominent lawyer. They were wed in January 1790. The Todds resided in a well-to-do neighborhood some distance from Dolley's family. Dolley soon had children—John Payne Todd (called Payne) in February 1792 and William Temple Todd in July 1793. Soon after William's birth, tragedy struck. Philadelphia suffered an outbreak of Yellow Fever that killed more than five thousand people, including John Todd and William. Widowed at the age of 25, Dolley struggled financially. Women could not lawfully own property at that time, and her husband's estate was withheld from her. Aaron Burr, an acquaintance, helped her by giving legal advice, and she was eventually granted the estate. In 1793, Philadelphia functioned as the national capital. Washington City was literally under construction. The city bustled with prominent men doing the business of the people, including the very well-known Virginian, James Madison. Madison was a national figure for his work writing the Constitution and the Bill of Rights. At forty-three years of age, Madison was still a bachelor. Very cerebral and politically brilliant but short and socially awkward, he preferred his books to people. Madison got his first glimpse of Dolley in the spring of 1794 as they passed each other in the street. He, by his own recollection, was smitten. For the next week, he sought to catch another glimpse of her. Aaron Buur formally introduced the couple. Within months, Madison proposed. They wed in May 1794 and moved to Montpelier, Madison's Virginia plantation. Over the years,

Dolley and James developed a loving partnership. He was a patient, loving stepfather, and Dolley was, socially, everything he was not.

When Thomas Jefferson was elected president in 1800, he appointed James Madison as Secretary of State. The Madison's took up residence in a modest house in Washington, where Dolley quickly inserted herself into the social fabric of the capital. At that time, Washington was a dismal place with few public buildings. The capital building was under construction; the executive residence newly completed, but there were very few roads or streets. A stream ran down the middle of Pennsylvania Avenue.

Still, it was the capital of the new republic, and as such, it buzzed with energy. At the dawn of the 19th century, many Americans were skeptical about the success of the Republic. Political culture and protocol had not yet fully developed, nor had a national identity. Americans were still New Yorkers, Virginians, and Pennsylvanians. As a result, politics was an ugly and, very often, violent business. The many brawls and duels between Federalists and Republicans are legendary. Jefferson brought to the executive residence his own peculiar Republican notions of how the President of the Republic should act, greet people, and behave. He was appalled that Washington and Adams before him emulated the courtly culture of England when greeting dignitaries and important people. Jefferson wanted the president to be a man of the people, as demonstrated in the infamous "Merry

Affair." Dolley, a keen observer of all things social, took to hosting events for Jefferson.

James Madison was elected president in 1808. In that year, the executive residence had no significance. It was thought of as simply the place where the president lived. It still had not been formally decorated or furnished. Dolley wanted it to be much more. She hired the architect Benjamin Latrobe to decorate and furnish the residence, giving it a uniquely American style. Greek and Roman designs symbolized that Americans were the inheritors of democracy and republic makers. Central to her design scheme was the placing of Gilbert Stuart's portrait of George Washington.

By this time, Dolley had already become a crucial element in the Washington's social circle. She made it her business to befriend the wives of foreign diplomats, Senators, and Congressmen. Her warm, vivacious personality endeared her to everyone she met. She even won over Mrs. Merry. Henry Clay once said to her, "Everyone loves Dolley Madison," to which she replied, "Because Dolley Madison loves everyone" (Klos 2013). With the executive residence decorated and furnished, Dolley set out to help her husband politically and to complete the development of American political culture.

Every Wednesday evening, Dolley hosted a dinner party at the executive residence. She made a point of inviting a good mix of diplomats, Federalists, Republicans, judges, and, of course, their wives. She created a warm social environment where men who, almost daily, brawled and dueled with each other in Congress could meet and discuss politics informally over ice cream, a luxurious dessert at that time. Her dinner parties were so popular they became known as the weekly "squeeze." Today in Washington and state capitals across the U.S., the bulk of politics is conducted in the same way. Dolley Madison created this enduring tradition. She became the public face of her husband's administration, and as such, she was the first to be called the First Lady. Moreover, the executive residence became known as the White House—a national home.

When British soldiers burned the capital, including the White House, in 1814, while the men ran away (including her husband, the President), Dolley had the presence of mind to save the portrait of Washington before fleeing. She had a profound appreciation for the importance of national symbols. Her act of defiance spared one of the few national symbols the young Republic could lay claim to. After the war, Washington City lay in ruins. Many congressmen wanted to abandon the capital for Philadelphia. The Madisons took up residence at the Octagon House, where Dolley wasted no time in preparing it to host her weekly squeeze. She spearheaded the movement to rebuild Washington rather than abandon it. Through her efforts, Washington survived, was rebuilt, and remains our capital still to this day.

Patriots, a time for reflection and action.

Today's gender studies curriculum falsely reinforces the concept of the patriarchal contempt of men towards women and how women were merely second-class citizens. While it is true women did not enjoy all the privileges of men at the time, most of the founders did respect the women in their lives. How is it that a lady of little means could rise to such prominence and importance to the nation? Dolley Madison's early years were filled with loss, heartbreak, and poverty. *Yet, she managed to do much more than many of the powerful men of her day.*

Dolley Madison was not a "social climber." She understood people, she listened, she respected, and she took the initiative to make things better when she saw the need. The fires of hell in the Washington City wasteland burning during the War of 1812 could not bring her bright, heavenly spirit down.

Too often, patriots of today are cynical and depressed, thinking, "The country is going to hell in a hand-basket." The idea of taking up a righteous cause in defense of their freedoms escapes them. Why persist in such negative reflection? Isn't it negativity that has brought us to the awful

state we now find ourselves in today? The American nation was built by men and women like Dolley Madison, who perceptively saw issues, pragmatically solved them, and led with grace, wisdom, and courage. We have much to learn from this National Treasure.

*Figure 21. Dolley Madison
(Purchased Alamy.com
23 Sept. 2022)*

Ka Duke Paoa
(Hawaiian—The Duke Paoa)

We Believe in Charity, Love, Respect, Kindness & living Aloha

he Hawaiian word "Aloha" is traditionally used to warmly welcome or to convey a fond and tender farewell to a loved one. The Spirit of Aloha is one of the warmest forms of love expressed by those who recognize its special power to connect people. Aloha's acceptance, welcoming harmony, and kindness has depth and pierces the hearts of souls, providing solace and a comforting embrace to those in desperate search of peace. If one allows it, Aloha's transformational power stays for life and creates a ripple effect as it diffuses to other souls in search of deep healing. The Spirit of Aloha is one of the closest forms of Divine love we can feel or sense here on earth. It is the greatest gift the islands have given to the world and to America. This story tells of Aloha's most memorable and important ambassador. His Aloha Spirit brought significant changes to race relations in the nation and brought exciting and novel changes to the world of professional sports.

***

POW! The firearm's report commenced the high-profile competition. The handsome, bronzed, and muscular young man hesitated a bit, fearing that he would disqualify himself by jumping too soon into the cool pool of water. Finally coming to his senses, he realized his moment had come! He dove into the water and displayed his remarkable gift as a swimmer for the enthralled audience. Stroke after freestyle stroke, he glided through the water in the 100-meter swimming heat. His initial hesitation put him in last place at the start of the race. But, no matter, he was born for this event. His body was perfectly attuned to the water, executing powerful swimming strokes and kicks, making his movements seem effortless. Soon, he passed most of his competitors. In the final heat, he outpaced the lead swimmer and easily won the race, tying the former world record at 1:02.4 minutes. This remarkable young man secured the Olympic gold medal for the United States, his first. The world-class athlete also represented his beloved land of Hawaii. The win propelled him into the world in unexpected ways and changed the world (Davis 2015).

Duke Paoa Kahinu Mokoe Hulikohola Kahanamoku (Duke Paoa Kahanamoku) was born in 1890 on the island of Oahu. Hailing from a large *ohana* (family), his family's financial means were poor in the little town of Honolulu. At the time of his birth, Hawaii was its own nation-state, ruled by a constitutional monarch, Queen Lili'uokalani. After many years of tension between the Queen and the U.S.

sugar business and agricultural interests in the islands, a coup deposed the monarch in 1893, making Hawaii a United States protectorate. Later, after the Spanish-American War in 1899, Congress voted for the island chain to become a territory of the United States as the realities of logistics to East Asia and the newly acquired formerly Spanish territories of Guam and the Philippines necessitated a naval presence in the Pacific. Duke inherited his U.S. citizenship through this fairly rapid course of events. Duke saw life dramatically change in the islands as the United States continued to gain more influence over the island chain.

Duke had street smarts but was not an engaged student. He dropped out of high school and worked as a laborer to support his family, honoring the sacred obligations to his *ohana*, which was sorely needed after the untimely passing of his father at 48 years old. However, Duke always found time to spend hours in the place he loved—the sea. Swimming, rowing outriggers, and especially surfing were treasured activities he took great pleasure in. His passion would lead him to become an international superstar. The fame came with a price, but Duke was the right person at the right time to change an important narrative and demonstrate Aloha and represent his new nation (Davis 2015).

Duke faced the shadow of racism with grace, on the islands and on the mainland. For example, when he was not permitted to join the prominent local clubs, this was no matter to him. He formed his own club where all were welcomed. When a prestigious swimming club's coach doubted his remarkable world-record-breaking swimming time, he simply accepted a challenge to prove himself. He swam again, forcing the coach to recognize his swimming prowess and talent. That recognition led to an offer to be on the 1912 U.S. Olympic Team in Norway, where he won his first of multiple Olympic medals in the succeeding 12 years. When challenges faced the Duke, he smiled and then subsequently beat them all.

Patriots, a time for reflection and action.

Hawaii is the most culturally and racially diverse of all the states. The islands are a gateway to Asia and the South Pacific. Hawaii is also of great strategic economic and military import. The islands' location enables the freedom of navigation of ocean-laden vessels throughout the world. Hawaii is the United States' most important line of defense against very real threats in the Pacific rim. Multiple military facilities dot its landscape. This includes the headquarters of the U.S. Indo-Pacific Combatant Command, the oldest and arguably the most significant Command, as it is responsible for defending and supporting national policy of about one fifth of the globe, more than any of the other geographic combatant commands. Hawaii's breezy trade winds brought generations of peoples of cultures from all over who have successfully mingled for generations. While no society can proclaim complete harmonious relations between the races, including Hawaii, the islanders demonstrate how Americans can live and support one another with a common belief in equality, liberty, respect, and living aloha.

Critics cry racism and proclaim the islands should be freed from the oppressive U.S. Hawaiians have legitimate concerns with regard to its history and affiliation with the United States. U.S. business interests deceptively and illegally deposed Queen Lili'uokalani. Today, purchasing property and living in Hawaii is very expensive and out of reach for many locals. Tourism, Hawaii's main industry, is a double-edged sword. Tourism brings money, but it also brings many problems, including crowding, traffic, and the degradation of the natural habitats which Hawaiians use to farm and fish. The life expectancy and health of the Native Hawaiian population are poor, with an average age of 62 ("Fewer Years" 2019). The secondary education system in Hawaii is unexceptional. Practical trade and technical schools are rare in the islands. Poor educational opportunities stifle *keiki* (children) opportunities to avoid poverty or merely just scrape by. Many locals choose to work for the military or in tourism service positions, as these are the main sources of regular employment. Indeed, life for locals is very, very challenging. More should be done to recognize their plight, as the Hawaiian people are important to our culture and nation.

However, comparatively, the standard of living for Hawaiians is better than what is found in neighboring Polynesian islands. Micronesia, Tonga, Samoa, Kiribati, and other island nations are in a worse position. Further, the Pacific islands are highly dependent on U.S. and foreign support to survive, unfortunately. Hawaiians also have the benefit of a handful of fine universities on the islands and have the benefit of going to school anywhere in the United States, should they choose. The Hawaiian state government, while heavy-handed in its policies, has made remarkable efforts to help protect the natural environment from overuse and abuse by ignorant tourists and locals alike. Other isles, such as Samoa, do not have such strict protections. The United States has made some recognition and concession to indicate the wrongs of the past. An example is President Grover Cleveland's strong denunciation of the 1893 coup, which occurred shortly before he took office, and President William Clinton's formal 1993 apology for the illegal coup ("1993" 2022). There is more to do, but the United States has made attempts to make things right.

Further, foregoing the Hawaiian Islands is not a practical or prudent option. This is not only true for national security reasons but also for practical reasons for locals. Other nations, such as China, make absolutely no efforts to accommodate or offer apologies from Chinese Communist Party officials to territories they have "acquired," such as Mongolia, Nepal, Tibet, Hong Kong, Macao, or the Uygur territories of Xianjing China. In fact, the Chinese Communist Party establishes "re-education camps" and prisons, practice organ harvesting, and horribly abuse those whom they have conquered. Today, observe how the Chinese Communist Party threatens Taiwan. Imagine the horror that would befall the Hawaiian people should the Communist Chinese Party occupy Hawaii. It is an unpleasant and frightening thought. The struggles Hawaiians face today would pale in comparison to the prospect or the specter of China.

Duke Kahanamoku's contribution to the nation was significant on many levels. He bridged a time of significant change for Hawaii and the nation. His humility and grace helped bring about racial equality. He was the precursor to the great Jackie Robinson of American Baseball fame. Duke also was the primary driving force that introduced surfing to the world, which is now a popular, internationally recognized sport and fun activity. His efforts helped him become a beloved international figure who admirably represented his island homeland and proudly represented the United States. He saved eight lives from a capsized vessel off the coast of California, paddling out to save them. He graciously served in efforts to support the troops during WWII in various capacities. Duke supported Hawaii's statehood. He served his community as a sheriff in his later years. While Duke evolved in a parallel course to Hawaii throughout the 20th century, he never disregarded or disrespected his Hawaiian cultural heritage. Instead, he celebrated it and helped integrate and infuse his culture, customs, and traditions into the American one. The poor local from Honolulu greatly added, perhaps unwittingly, but most certainly, to the American experience with grace and with Aloha.

Further, Duke's Aloha Spirit led to a Hawaiian patriotism for the United States. The shared experience of the attack on Pearl Harbor in 1941 strengthened the bonds throughout the islands. One of Hawaii's homegrown heroes is Senator Daniel Inouye, a Hawaiian of Japanese ancestry and Medal of Honor recipient who served honorable in WWII in the 442 Infantry Regiment (comprised of other Japanese Hawaiians, many of whom whose parents were detained in camps after Pearl Harbor). Senator Inouye lost an arm serving the United States but was never bitter. He continued to serve as the first U.S. Representative of Hawaii post-state-hood in 1959 and had a long, distinguished career as a U.S. Senator. Another local hero is former Congressional U.S. Representative and former presidential candidate Tulsi Gabbard. Representative Gabbard has also served honorably in Middle East battlefields and Africa and still serves as a Lt. Colonel in the U.S. Army Reserve. Duke's legacy greatly contributed to steering the islands to support the United States throughout significant changes during his lifetime. The Duke's efforts produced a stronger, more resilient American nation.

Figure 22. Duke Paoa Kahanamoku (Purchased Alamy.com 23 Sept. 2022)

Citizenship

"Where there is no vision, the people perish: but he that keepeth the law, happy is he." Proverbs 29:18

Key Takeaways, Actions for You

Teach and practice gratitude in your personal life and home.

People who practice gratitude are generally happier and healthier. A "woe is me" or "the country is lost" mindset does little and means less. Reflect and be grateful for what you have every morning, the blessings that liberty has provided, and ponder on how these have made a difference in your life daily. Think of life without those blessings, and contemplate what you would do to continue, in gratitude, to support those blessings. Perhaps you can start traditions of gratitude in your home and life. For example, during Thanksgiving, read aloud President George Washington's proclamation on the First Thanksgiving to your families before your Thanksgiving meal. Also, learn about the gratitude that our founders and people expressed throughout our history. For example, discover tidbits of historical facts, such as how the words *"Laus Deo,"* Latin for "Praise be to God," are inscribed on the Washington Monument.

Have faith, find your purpose, and expect miracles.

As the old and the wise reflect on life, many discover that "things," good and bad, happen for a reason. The Founding Father Samuel Adams had a host of unhappy breaks in life. These included the loss of his beloved first wife, a failure in business, detention and harassment by the British officials in colonial Massachusetts, the regulatory British government stifling his successful father's businesses to the point where he could barely survive, and resulted in protesting the British government in colonial halls on behalf of the oppressed people of Boston and Massachusetts. Despite this, Samuel Adams had great conviction that the colonies could separate from Britain and rule themselves. Indeed, he envisioned American Independence far before many of his colleagues and friends. Adams found his purpose in life, made important connections with like-minded souls, and successfully led efforts to declare independence from Britain. Samuel Adams became the metaphorical "glue" that brought the delegation of 55 men together in agreement on the radical course of action. Finally, his tireless efforts as an Anti-federalist ensured the codification of the Bill of Rights to the Constitution. His faith and steadfast purpose brought about the miracle of the United States of America. You are encouraged to draw closer to your Creator, reflect on your personal role, and act and witness what will unfold before you.

Find and develop your talents.

Closely linked to finding your purpose is developing your talents. Dr. Benjamin Franklin, a man of many talents, acted and refined his abilities, always engaging himself to be more and be better. As a scientist, he developed marvelous and meaningful inventions that have relevance to this day. For example, Franklin invented the lightning rod, which helped prevent the burning of villages and cities during lightning storms. He also invented bifocal glasses, swimming fins, the iron Franklin Stove to heat frigid homes, the urinary catheter, and the hauntingly beautiful musical instrument, the Armonica—his favorite invention. Further, he advanced humanity through his scientific pursuits with his studies on electricity. His efforts earned him international acclaim and a doctoral degree. Keep in mind the aforementioned are only his *scientific* achievements. Dr. Franklin was a marvelously successful diplomat. His nearly single-handed efforts in France secured the alliance between the colonists and France; the King of France provided the desperately needed funding for the Glorious Cause. Further, he was a successful printer, a witty and clever writer, the founder of a local fire company in Philadelphia, the first U.S. Postal Service General Postmaster, and a wise statesman. We may not all be Dr. Benjamin Franklins with "ten talents." However, each of us has at least "one talent." Let us use the talent for good to secure the blessings of liberty and defend them. There is no need to hide the talent in a nation that allows for such personal development and progress.

Stand for Old Glory; be a standard bearer.

A recent article in Veteran.com is exceptionally disappointing. The article entitled "Top Reasons Gen Z Should Join the Military" highlights reasons for joining in an effort to boost pitiful recruitment. Referencing Forbes Magazine, the article defines Gen Z as "… those who were born between 1995 and the year 2010, and *describes* the typical Generation Z citizen as being more competitive, better at multitasking than Millennials, and ready for *independence*" (Military Benefits 2020). Yet, the article goes on to describe that Gen Z should join the military for (1) education benefits, (2) health care, (3) technical training, and (4) financial stability. So, a generation purportedly ready for "independence" should join a time-honored profession and become *dependent* on the government?

What is wrong with this picture?

Well, this line of reasoning emphasizes that a candidate for military service should focus on what *they can get from the military/government* as opposed to the noble cause of *pieatas*—for love and duty to God, neighbor, and nation—and for adventure and character building. The article goes against the traditions embodied by President John F. Kennedy's famous quote, "Ask not what your country can do for you, ask what you can do for your country."

We need standard bearers to lead and promote patriotism. While the efforts in the above-referenced article are targeted at recruiting (all branches of the military desperately need the new recruits, especially in this foolish, woke era), the ad completely misses the mark. Learn the ways of pieatas, pass it down to the younger generations, and learn and lead.

Take courage—fear is normal, but courage is not.

It is up to you to elect the best, the wisest, the honest, the courageous, and the fearless. Break the bonds that chain you to a system that makes you a feudal serf in the globalists' tyrannical game. Wise and good men and women arise and be engaged at all levels to overturn the tyranny we now face. _Not with arms, not with the storming of buildings like the capital in Washington DC. No!_ Do not let them provoke you to violence! The elite greatly desire this to use as an excuse to destroy you. The powerful salivate as they justify in their treacherous minds their power grab while simultaneously placating the masses, speaking with forked tongues, and sprinkling honey-soothing words like "democracy," "justice," and "rights" into their warped speeches or the devaluing of words once proudly spoken like "Patriot," which now is equated with militia groups.

Rather, advance with wisdom, critical thinking, knowledge, leadership, the pen which is mightier than the sword, your voice, and faith in your Creator to exercise your rights, exercising civil disobedience and self-defense only where necessary. As a wise dissident once noted, "The line separating good and evil passes not through states, nor between classes, nor between political parties either—but right through the human heart—and through all human hearts. This line shifts" (Holmquist 2018). Be wary of letting the line shift in your heart.

It is a nefarious tactic that one side can use violence to justify their political ends and, in the process, destroy lives, cities, and businesses in the name of "justice." While weaponized legalism attempts to quash the Spirit of Liberty, it will not succeed as the ideas of agency and freedom are eternal. Remember, the colonists resisted armed conflict until that fateful day in Lexington on April 19, 1775. We will be spit on. We will be derided. Some of us will be fired from our employers. Others will be assaulted physically, and our blood may be spilled. Some of us may be jailed. And yes, when all other tactics fail for our adversaries, the nuclear option in their lexicon against patriots will be unleashed with a maddening flurry—we will be called "racist."

Understand, this will happen no matter what. Why be afraid, especially when it is not true?

Learn to read, write, and reason with critical thinking.

In the Mel Gibson movie *Braveheart*, a movie that movingly celebrates a man's fight for freedom, there is a powerful scene between a young William Wallace, played by James Robinson, and his wealthy, stately, and wise Uncle Argyle, played by Brian Cox. Young William, with tear stains streaming on his mud-stained face, is freshly grieving the burial of his family after their murder at the hands of the deceptive King Longshanks of England. In the faint fire-lit room of his late parents' hut, the orphaned William admires and handles his uncle's sword. The shiny, steely weapon is almost as tall as the boy. The blade appeals to young William's baser instincts of hate and revenge. Perceptively reading young William's thoughts, Argyle Wallace takes his sword back and poignantly states, "First, learn to use this," tapping the indigent lad on the forehead and pointing to his brain. "Then, I'll teach you how to use this," before sheathing his sword.

In the modern era, we have teachers and classical thinkers who exhort the same. Dr. Jordan Peterson noted, "… to learn critical thinking one must learn to write. If you can think, speak, and write, you are absolutely deadly. There is nothing that can stop you" (Bite-Sized Philosophy 2017, 0:04:01). It's the most powerful weapon you can learn. It takes discipline, but your freedom is worth the effort! Learn debate, logic, critical thinking, and reason, the classical virtues that our founders learned. Learn and teach the difference between beauty and baseness as our ancestors and the ancients of Greece and Rome did.

Support the military, law enforcement, and first responders every chance you get.

Active-Duty component military service members frequently move, are called away to long deployments, and are frequently training. Reserve component military members are expected to gain and maintain the same qualifications as

Active-Duty counterparts, must maintain a civilian career in addition to their military one, support their families, and are subject to lengthy recall at any time. While there are good benefits, these sacrifices take their toll on family life and marriages, yet the military men and women persist so with reverence and honor for the nation. Not only are military members willing to lay down their lives for God, nation, and neighbor/family in physical battle, they sacrifice much of their life in study and training.

Local law enforcement has extreme challenges too. Most in American society do not know what it is like to wear body armor to work and not know if they will be violently harmed on any given day. Further, many do not appreciate the emotional strain law enforcement work puts on them. Many optimistic, young believers in public service grow to be old and cynical after years of dealing with the criminal mind and lenient judges who perpetuate the revolving doors of justice. Yet, we have a celebrated criminal class that gleefully chants, "Pigs in a blanket, fry 'em like bacon," with true intent to cause maximum harm and weaken our communities. Many vicious police deaths and injuries have been tied to this ruthless underclass. Back the blue, and support local law enforcement by giving to charities or participating in events that support them and their families. The same applies to first responders, Emergency Medical Technicians, and Firefighters. Sadly, their uniforms make them a target, too, for those who feign love but openly hate and destroy. Like local law enforcement, first responders are a crucial part of our communities, towns, counties, cities, and states. They need our moral and financial support too.

Recognize Every Life has Value, Reject Racism. Men & Women are Equal.

Robert K. Thomas and Shirly Wilkes Thomas insightfully observed, "During recent years, most of us have been made increasingly aware of the plight of minority groups, but, once again, we often need look no further than our own families to find instructive parallels that test our commitment to the unselfishness that is a hallmark of patriotism. Can we honestly say that the youngest child in our home is neither bullied nor shamed by his older brothers and sisters? It is an easy step from insisting that a small brother not tag along because he is 'too little' and would therefore need special care, to discriminating against those apparently disadvantaged by race, sex, or age who need extraordinary consideration if they are to compete successfully. When we are able to make each family member feel equally loved and equally important—and we do this by acknowledging the smallest contribution and honoring the greatest need—we all develop a concept of loyalty and concern that will transfer easily from home to country. If, in the family, we have learned to be tolerant of difference and generous in judgment, we find it easier to work with others outside the family circle in democratic goodwill. Research in child development suggests that cooperation and concern for others are usually learned before children begin the first grade. If they are not learned in the home, they will be hard to find in the school yard, on the campus, or on the job" (Thomas and Thomas 1976).

Engage in participatory citizenship.

Engaging is no longer an option. The academic intelligencia, the media, tech, and big business executives, the permanent political class, and the judiciary that leniently and even vocally support the perpetually aggrieved have nothing to show except destruction, force, and bondage. These so-called thought "leaders" and "influencers" possibly have, on average, a higher "intelligence quotient." Most certainly, the intelligencia have inscribed pieces of fancy paper that say they are smart. However, that does not give them a deistic "right to rule." As demonstrated in recent years, while intelligent, their *wisdom quotient* hovers around zero. Do not fool yourselves or let them fool you into believing this class are leaders; they are far from it. The *paideia* that has enveloped their lives has *failed* to teach them wisdom and virtue. Put another way, they are highly intelligent people *with absolutely nothing to offer.* Remember, the socialist experiments they promote have failed again and again.

The comforts that freedom has brought you and *made you soft* are now rapidly fading away. You have been lulled away into security, but are you now awake? Like the minutemen in colonial Massachusetts and the Continentals in New York, you are called on to stand and fight to rebuild a Federated Constitutional Republic. Failure in this cause is not an option. Victory in freedom is the noblest of causes. We must gather and unite, or our nation or our liberties will surely wither, relegating you to serfdom. Participatory citizenship is the key. Voting and being active in the process are exceptionally important. For remember, "The accumulation of all powers, legislative, executive, and judiciary, in the same hands, whether of one, a few, or many, and whether hereditary, self-appointed, or elective, may justly be pronounced the very definition of tyranny" – James Madison (Madison 1788).

Beware of the elitists and soothsayers who will destroy you.

Do not trust the permanent political class, or the technocratic elites. They have lied to you for years, and more importantly, they have failed you. They aim to take your freedoms, "You will own nothing, and you will be happy" is their motto (Darrell Vermilion 2020, 0:01:32). However, what they intentionally neglect to tell you is they will control what you can and cannot do, where you can and cannot go, how you can travel, and what you must do to remain in their good graces. That, my countrymen, is bondage.

The American-born Julie Inman Grant, who now operates as the Australian government's eSafety Commissioner (who is also a World Economic Forum member and former Microsoft and Twitter employee), in May 2022 proclaimed, "We are finding ourselves in a place where we have increasing polarization everywhere, and everything feels binary when it doesn't need to be … So, I think we're going to have to think about a recalibration of a whole range of human rights that are playing out online, from the freedom of speech to be[ing] free from online violence" (Klausica Schwabescu 2022, 0:00:26).

At the gathering of a powerful cartel in Davos, Switzerland, Dr. Ngaire Woods openly admitted at the January 2022 World Economic Forum (WEF) conference, "The good news is that [we] the elite (yes, they arrogantly call themselves that), across the world trust each other more and more, so we can design and do beautiful things together. The bad news is that in every single country that we were polling, the majority of people trust us less and less. So, we can lead, but if people aren't following we're not going to get to where *we* want to go" (emphasis added) (Scallan 2022).

The New Zealand-born, Oxford elitist is correct. We do not trust them. We are a free people, not subjects to the elite or the intellectual elite who act as deity incarnate. We, the people, have *no obligation* to, nor shall we become pawns in their "beautiful things," their treacherous designs.

Don't just learn virtue, be virtuous.

The Founding Fathers subscribed to the Greek philosopher Aristotle's view of virtue. True happiness is achieved when the soul and virtue align. Citizens who practice living a life of virtue and reason contribute to establishing an American Republic built on virtue. Anciently, philosophers taught the most important virtues included wisdom, justice, moderation, and courage, with courage being the most important because courage defends the others. We could add and modernize the virtue list to include gratitude, as it helps us remember who we are, where we came from, and our fortunes and helps us to live a life of wonder and awe as opposed to bitterness and bile. The founders created the Declaration of Independence and the Constitution as instruments to support virtuous living and virtuous government.

To support the undergirding virtuous infrastructure of the nation, we, too, need to have virtue. If you have addictions to substances, drugs, alcohol, or pornography, please seek help to overcome them. For it is vital for you this day to join this battle and be able to have your senses and wits sharp to be able to decern between truth and error, wrong and right, and good and evil. It is crucial that you develop into happy warriors. Strengthen your families. Be serving, be charitable, be loving, be kind, but also be firm in your beliefs. It takes an awful lot of work and discipline, but think virtuously. Rome is burning. Your mind, your heart, and your soul need to be aligned as we quench the fires.

Support local, free market capitalism, and reject socialism.

From the Pilgrims landing to the Westward expansion self-reliance proved invaluable, a trait we have largely forgotten as government has tried to implement cradle-to-grave benefits. Entrepreneurs and business owners who fight the odds and make or provide something of value are treasured gifts that should be nourished and supported. They are practicing a self-reliant mindset. As for the government, Thomas Jefferson rightly noted, "A wise and frugal government, which shall leave men free to regulate their own pursuits of industry and improvement, and shall not take from the mouth of labor the bread it has earned—this is the sum of good government" (Jefferson 1801). James Madison noted, "Government is instituted to protect property of every sort; as well that which lies in the various rights of individuals, as that which the term particularly expresses. This being the end of government, that alone is a just government which impartially secures to every man whatever is his own" (Madison 1792).

Live Aloha and practice charity to strengthen your communities.

We are an isolated people today. In years past, friends and neighbors would gather at bowling alleys, churches, bars or pubs, or at community halls or even personal homes to play games, read books, or worship and have fun. The sense of community has been lost and certainly stifled even more since the COVID-19 pandemic and the advent of gaming and streaming video services.

With an eye towards community and charity, reach out and chat with people in your community. Develop a deep sense of empathy to aid and support your fellow citizens and neighbors. Volunteer to teach something of value. Serve in your houses of worship, your neighborhoods, and your communities. Gather and connect with others. Perhaps you can serve in shelters or soup kitchens to remind you and your family of your blessings. Visit the widows and widowers.

Even better, engage or support services or activities that help people get out of poverty and become self-reliant. As Dr. Benjamin Franklin (1766) noted, "I am for doing good to the poor, but ... I think the best way of doing good to the poor, is not making them easy in poverty, but leading or driving them out of it" (On the Price of Corn and Management of the Poor). Thomas Jefferson (1787) noted, "Dependence begets subservience and venality, suffocates the germ of virtue, and prepares fit tools for the designs of ambition" (Notes on the State of Virginia).

As much as politicians and unelected bodies claim they can solve all your problems and make you happy, the hard reality is they cannot. At that level, there are too many regulations and far too many variables to manage. Meaningful change can only happen through local action and learning to care for and support your families and your communities through loving service.

Like Samuel Adams accomplished with his kin and friends, nourish bonds with family, and wisely choose and reinforce friendships that strengthen you, your family, your community, state, and nation. Choose those who you would put your life on the line for, and who would do the same for you. Ties like this saved Samuel Adams from capture and certain death multiple times, and are the same bonds that make law enforcement and the military effective.

Reclaim your voice. Mastery takes time.

Consistent action in all you learn from this work takes time to internalize and master. Do not be afraid, discouraged, or give up. Great and important things take persistence and time. In your persistent actions you can be a beacon to proclaim and virtually fly the title of liberty in defense of your family, your faith, and your Creator's given freedoms. Remember, your rights are not derived from government. We, the people, are in charge, and only by our consent are we governed. Let these be our rallying cry, our own Title of Liberty.

Using truth, honor and defend your nation, customs, culture, and traditions. Let us honor and defend the Founding Fathers, Declaration of Independence, and U.S. Constitution using truth to reawaken the American Spirit! Share this work and discuss it! Celebrate the 4th of July, Thanksgiving, Hannukah, or Christmas. Remember the veterans on Veterans' Day and those who died defending your freedoms on Memorial Day. Teach the importance of these traditions to help us remember who we are! Choose, this day, to breathe the air of freedom!

Come, come, ye Patriots, Ye Free Americans, no toil nor labor fear
Behold, the battle sight
Why should we think to earn a great reward
If we now shun the fight?
Gird up your loins, fresh courage take,
Our God will never us forsake
And soon we'll have this tale to tell
All is well! All is well!

(Adaptation of William Clayton's "All is Well" or "Come, Come, Ye Saints", 1846)

The Declaration of Independence

In Congress, July 4, 1776

The unanimous Declaration of the thirteen united States of America, When in the Course of human events, it becomes necessary for one people to dissolve the political bands which have connected them with another, and to assume among the powers of the earth, the separate and equal station to which the Laws of Nature and of Nature's God entitle them, a decent respect to the opinions of mankind requires that they should declare the causes which impel them to the separation.

We hold these truths to be self-evident, that all men are created equal, that they are endowed by their Creator with certain unalienable Rights, that among these are Life, Liberty and the pursuit of Happiness.—That to secure these rights, Governments are instituted among Men, deriving their just powers from the consent of the governed, —That whenever any Form of Government becomes destructive of these ends, it is the Right of the People to alter or to abolish it, and to institute new Government, laying its foundation on such principles and organizing its powers in such form, as to them shall seem most likely to effect their Safety and Happiness. Prudence, indeed, will dictate that Governments long established should not be changed for light and transient causes; and accordingly all experience hath shewn, that mankind are more disposed to suffer, while evils are sufferable, than to right themselves by abolishing the forms to which they are accustomed. But when a long train of abuses and usurpations, pursuing invariably the same Object evinces a design to reduce them under absolute Despotism, it is their right, it is their duty, to throw off such Government, and to provide new Guards for their future security.—Such has been the patient sufferance of these Colonies; and such is now the necessity which constrains them to alter their former Systems of Government. The history of the present King of Great Britain is a history of repeated injuries and usurpations, all having in direct object the establishment of an absolute Tyranny over these States. To prove this, let Facts be submitted to a candid world.

He has refused his Assent to Laws, the most wholesome and necessary for the public good.

He has forbidden his Governors to pass Laws of immediate and pressing importance, unless suspended in their operation till his Assent should be obtained; and when so suspended, he has utterly neglected to attend to them.

He has refused to pass other Laws for the accommodation of large districts of people, unless those people would relinquish the right of Representation in the Legislature, a right inestimable to them and formidable to tyrants only.

He has called together legislative bodies at places unusual, uncomfortable, and distant from the depository of their public Records, for the sole purpose of fatiguing them into compliance with his measures.

He has dissolved Representative Houses repeatedly, for opposing with manly firmness his invasions on the rights of the people. He has refused for a long time, after such dissolutions, to cause others to be elected; whereby the Legislative powers, incapable of Annihilation, have returned to the People at large for their exercise; the State remaining in the mean time exposed to all

the dangers of invasion from without, and convulsions within. He has endeavoured to prevent the population of these States; for that purpose obstructing the Laws for Naturalization of Foreigners; refusing to pass others to encourage their migrations hither, and raising the conditions of new Appropriations of Lands.

He has obstructed the Administration of Justice, by refusing his Assent to Laws for establishing Judiciary powers.

He has made Judges dependent on his Will alone, for the tenure of their offices, and the amount and payment of their salaries.

He has erected a multitude of New Offices, and sent hither swarms of Officers to harass our people, and eat out their substance.

He has kept among us, in times of peace, Standing Armies without the Consent of our legislatures.

He has affected to render the Military independent of and superior to the Civil power.

He has combined with others to subject us to a jurisdiction foreign to our constitution, and unacknowledged by our laws; giving his Assent to their Acts of pretended Legislation:

For Quartering large bodies of armed troops among us:

For protecting them, by a mock Trial, from punishment for any Murders which they should commit on the Inhabitants of these States:

For cutting off our Trade with all parts of the world: For imposing Taxes on us without our Consent:

For depriving us in many cases, of the benefits of Trial by Jury:

For transporting us beyond Seas to be tried for pretended offences

For abolishing the free System of English Laws in a neighbouring Province, establishing therein an Arbitrary government, and enlarging its Boundaries so as to render it at once an example and fit instrument for introducing the same absolute rule into these Colonies:

For taking away our Charters, abolishing our most valuable Laws, and altering fundamentally the Forms of our Governments: For suspending our own Legislatures, and declaring themselves invested with power to legislate for us in all cases whatsoever.

He has abdicated Government here, by declaring us out of his Protection and waging War against us.

He has plundered our seas, ravaged our Coasts, burnt our towns, and destroyed the lives of our people.

He is at this time transporting large Armies of foreign Mercenaries to compleat the works of death, desolation and tyranny, already begun with circumstances of Cruelty & perfidy scarcely paralleled in the most barbarous ages, and totally unworthy the Head of a civilized nation.

He has constrained our fellow Citizens taken Captive on the high Seas to bear Arms against their Country, to become the executioners of their friends and Brethren, or to fall themselves by their Hands.

He has excited domestic insurrections amongst us, and has endeavoured to bring on the inhabitants of our frontiers, the merciless Indian Savages, whose known rule of warfare, is an undistinguished destruction of all ages, sexes and conditions.

In every stage of these Oppressions We have Petitioned for Redress in the most humble terms: Our repeated Petitions have been answered only by repeated injury. A Prince whose character is thus marked by every act which may define a Tyrant, is unfit to be the ruler of a free people.

Nor have We been wanting in attentions to our Brittish brethren. We have warned them from time to time of attempts by their legislature to extend an unwarrantable jurisdiction over us. We have reminded them of the circumstances of our emigration and settlement here. We have appealed to their native justice and magnanimity, and we have conjured them by the ties of our common kindred to disavow these usurpations, which, would inevitably interrupt our connections and correspondence. They too have been deaf to the voice of justice and of consanguinity. We must, therefore, acquiesce in the necessity, which denounces our Separation, and hold them, as we hold the rest of mankind, Enemies in War, in Peace Friends.

We, therefore, the Representatives of the united States of America, in General Congress, Assembled, appealing to the Supreme Judge of the world for the rectitude of our intentions, do, in the Name, and by Authority of the good People of these Colonies, solemnly publish and declare, That these United Colonies are, and of Right ought to be Free and Independent States; that they are Absolved from all Allegiance to the British Crown, and that all political connection between them and the State of Great Britain, is and ought to be totally dissolved; and that as Free and Independent States, they have full Power to levy War, conclude Peace, contract Alliances, establish Commerce, and to do all other Acts and Things which Independent States may of right do. And for the support of this Declaration, with a firm reliance on the protection of divine Providence, we mutually pledge to each other our Lives, our Fortunes and our sacred Honor.

The Constitution of the United States

Adopted, September 17, 1787

Vermont (final state to ratify) January 10, 1791

PREAMBLE

We the People of the United States, in Order to form a more perfect Union, establish Justice, insure domestic Tranquility, provide for the common defense, promote the general Welfare, and secure the Blessings of Liberty to ourselves and our Posterity, do ordain and establish this Constitution for the United States of America.

Article I.

THE LEGISLATIVE BRANCH

Section 1. All legislative Powers herein granted shall be vested in a Congress of the United States, which shall consist of a Senate and House of Representatives.

THE HOUSE OF REPRESENTATIVES

Section 2. [1] The House of Representatives shall be composed of Members chosen every second Year by the People of the several States, and the Electors in each State shall have the Qualifications requisite for Electors of the most numerous Branch of the State Legislature.

[2] No Person shall be a Representative who shall not have attained to the Age of twenty-five Years, and been seven Years a Citizen of the United States, and who shall not, when elected, be an Inhabitant of that State in which he shall be chosen.

[3] [Representatives and direct Taxes shall be apportioned among the several States which may be included within this Union, according to their respective Numbers, which shall be determined by adding to the whole Number of free Persons, including those bound to Service for a Term of Years, and excluding Indians not taxed, three fifths of all other Persons.] (Note: Changed by section 2 of the Fourteenth Amendment.) The actual Enumeration shall

be made within three Years after the first Meeting of the Congress of the United States, and within every subsequent Term of ten Years, in such Manner as they shall by Law direct. The Number of Representatives shall not exceed one for every thirty Thousand, but each State shall have at Least one Representative; and until such enumeration shall be made, the State of New Hampshire shall be entitled to chuse three, Massachusetts eight, Rhode-Island and Providence Plantations one, Connecticut five, New-York six, New Jersey four, Pennsylvania eight, Delaware one, Maryland six, Virginia ten, North Carolina five, South Carolina five, and Georgia three.

[4] When vacancies happen in the Representation from any state, the Executive Authority thereof shall issue Writs of Election to fill such Vacancies.

[5] The House of Representatives shall chuse their Speaker and other Officers; and shall have the sole Power of Impeachment.

THE SENATE

Section 3. [1] The Senate of the United States shall be composed of two Senators from each State, [chosen by the Legislature thereof,] (Note: Changed by section 1 of the Seventeenth Amendment.) for six Years; and each Senator shall have one Vote.

[2] Immediately after they shall be assembled in Consequence of the first Election, they shall be divided as equally as may be into three Classes. The Seats of the Senators of the first Class shall be

vacated at the Expiration of the second Year, of the second Class at the Expiration of the fourth Year, and of the third Class at the Expiration of the sixth Year, so that one-third may be chosen every second Year; [and if Vacancies happen by Resignation, or otherwise, during the Recess of the Legislature of any State, the Executive thereof may make temporary Appointments until the next Meeting of the Legislature, which shall then fill such Vacancies.] (Note: Changed by clause 2 of the Seventeenth Amendment.)

[3] No Person shall be a Senator who shall not have attained to the Age of thirty Years, and been nine Years a Citizen of the United States, and who shall not, when elected, be an Inhabitant of that State for which he shall be chosen.

[4] The Vice President of the United States shall be President of the Senate, but shall have no Vote, unless they be equally divided.

[5] The Senate shall chuse their other Officers, and also a President pro tempore, in the Absence of the Vice President, or when he shall exercise the Office of President of the United States.

[6] The Senate shall have the sole Power to try all Impeachments. When sitting for that Purpose, they shall be on Oath or Affirmation. When the President of the United States is tried, the Chief Justice shall preside: And no Person shall be convicted without the Concurrence of two thirds of the Members present.

[7] Judgment in Cases of Impeachment shall not extend further than to removal from Office, and

disqualification to hold and enjoy any Office of honor, Trust or Profit under the United States: but the Party convicted shall nevertheless be liable and subject to Indictment, Trial, Judgment and Punishment, according to Law.

THE ORGANIZATION OF CONGRESS

Section 4. [1] The Times, Places and Manner of holding Elections for Senators and Representatives, shall be prescribed in each State by the Legislature thereof; but the Congress may at any time by Law make or alter such Regulations, except as to the Place of Chusing Senators.

[2] The Congress shall assemble at least once in every Year, and such Meeting shall be [on the first Monday in December,] (Note: Changed by section 2 of the Twentieth Amendment.) unless they shall by Law appoint a different Day.

Section 5. [1] Each House shall be the Judge of the Elections, Returns and Qualifications of its own Members, and a Majority of each shall constitute a Quorum to do Business; but a smaller number may adjourn from day to day, and may be authorized to compel the Attendance of absent Members, in such Manner, and under such Penalties as each House may provide.

[2] Each House may determine the Rules of its Proceedings, punish its Members for disorderly Behavior, and, with the Concurrence of two thirds, expel a Member.

[3] Each House shall keep a Journal of its Proceedings, and from time to time publish the same, excepting such Parts as may in their Judgment require Secrecy; and the Yeas and Nays of the Members of either House on any question shall, at the Desire of one fifth of those Present, be entered on the Journal.

[4] Neither House, during the Session of Congress, shall, without the Consent of the other, adjourn for more than three days, nor to any other Place than that in which the two Houses shall be sitting.

Section 6. [1] The Senators and Representatives shall receive a Compensation for their Services, to be ascertained by Law, and paid out of the Treasury of the United States. They shall in all Cases, except Treason, Felony and Breach of the Peace, be privileged from Arrest during their Attendance at the Session of their respective Houses, and in going to and returning from the same; and for any Speech or Debate in either House, they shall not be questioned in any other Place.

[2] No Senator or Representative shall, during the Time for which he was elected, be appointed to any civil Office under the Authority of the United States, which shall have been created, or the Emoluments whereof shall have been encreased during such time; and no Person holding any Office under the United States, shall be a Member of either House during his Continuance in Office.

Section 7. [1] All Bills for raising Revenue shall originate in the House of Representatives; but the Senate may propose or concur with Amendments as on other Bills.

[2] Every Bill which shall have passed the House of Representatives and the Senate, shall, before it become a Law, be presented to the President of the United States; If he approve he shall sign it, but if not he shall return it, with his Objections to that House in which it shall have originated, who shall enter the Objections at large on their Journal, and proceed to reconsider it. If after such Reconsideration two thirds of that House shall agree to pass the Bill, it shall be sent, together with the Objections, to the other House, by which it shall likewise be reconsidered, and if approved by two thirds of that House, it shall become a Law. But in all such Cases the Votes of both Houses shall be determined by Yeas and Nays, and the Names of the Persons voting for and against the Bill shall be entered on the Journal of each House respectively. If any Bill shall not be returned by the President within ten Days (Sundays excepted) after it shall have been presented to him, the Same shall be a Law, in like Manner as if he had signed it, unless the Congress by their Adjournment prevent its Return, in which Case it shall not be a Law.

[3] Every Order, Resolution, or Vote to which the Concurrence of the Senate and House of Representatives may be necessary (except on a question of Adjournment) shall be presented to the President of the United States; and before the Same shall take Effect, shall be approved by him, or being disapproved by him, shall be repassed by two thirds of the Senate and House of Representatives, according to the Rules and Limitations prescribed in the Case of a Bill.

POWERS GRANTED TO CONGRESS

Section 8. [1] The Congress shall have Power To lay and collect Taxes, Duties, Imposts and Excises, to pay the Debts and provide for the common Defence and general Welfare of the United States; but all Duties, Imposts and Excises shall be uniform throughout the United States;

[2] To borrow money on the credit of the United States;

[3] To regulate Commerce with foreign Nations, and among the several States, and with the Indian Tribes;

[4] To establish an uniform Rule of Naturalization, and uniform Laws on the subject of Bankruptcies throughout the United States;

[5] To coin Money, regulate the Value thereof, and of foreign Coin, and fix the Standard of Weights and Measures;

[6] To provide for the Punishment of counterfeiting the Securities and current Coin of the United States;

[7] To establish Post Offices and post Roads;

[8] To promote the Progress of Science and useful Arts, by securing for limited Times to Authors and Inventors the exclusive Right to their respective Writings and Discoveries;

[9] To constitute Tribunals inferior to the supreme Court;

[10] To define and punish Piracies and Felonies committed on the high Seas, and Offenses against the Law of Nations;

[11] To declare War, grant Letters of Marque and Reprisal, and make Rules concerning Captures on Land and Water;

[12] To raise and support Armies, but no Appropriation of Money to that Use shall be for a longer Term than two Years;

[13] To provide and maintain a Navy;

[14] To make Rules for the Government and Regulation of the land and naval Forces;

[15] To provide for calling forth the Militia to execute the Laws of the Union, suppress Insurrections and repel Invasions;

[16] To provide for organizing, arming, and disciplining the Militia, and for governing such Part of them as may be employed in the Service of the United States, reserving to the States respectively, the Appointment of the Officers, and the Authority of training the Militia according to the discipline prescribed by Congress;

[17] To exercise exclusive Legislation in all Cases whatsoever, over such District (not exceeding ten Miles square) as may, by Cession of particular States, and the acceptance of Congress, become the Seat of the Government of the United States, and to exercise like Authority over all Places purchased by the Consent of the Legislature of the State in which the Same shall be, for the Erection of Forts, Magazines, Arsenals, dock-Yards, and other needful Buildings; —And

[18] To make all Laws which shall be necessary and proper for carrying into Execution the foregoing Powers, and all other Powers vested by this Constitution in the Government of the United States, or in any Department or Officer thereof.

POWER FORBIDDEN TO CONGRESS

Section 9. [1] The Migration or Importation of such Persons as any of the States now existing shall think proper to admit, shall not be prohibited by the Congress prior to the Year one thousand eight hundred and eight, but a tax or duty may be imposed on such Importation, not exceeding ten dollars for each Person.

[2] The privilege of the Writ of Habeas Corpus shall not be suspended, unless when in Cases of Rebellion or Invasion the public Safety may require it.

[3] No Bill of Attainder or ex post facto Law shall be passed.

[4] No Capitation, or other direct, Tax shall be laid, unless in Proportion to the Census or Enumeration herein before directed to be taken. (Note: See the Sixteenth Amendment.)

[5] No Tax or Duty shall be laid on Articles exported from any State.

[6] No Preference shall be given by any Regulation of Commerce or Revenue to the Ports of one State over those of another: nor shall Vessels bound to, or from, one State, be obliged to enter, clear, or pay Duties in another.

[7] No Money shall be drawn from the Treasury, but in Consequence of Appropriations made by Law; and a regular Statement and Account of the Receipts and Expenditures of all public Money shall be published from time to time.

[8] No Title of Nobility shall be granted by the United States: And no Person holding any Office of Profit or Trust under

them, shall, without the Consent of the Congress, accept of any present, Emolument, Office, or Title, of any kind whatever, from any King, Prince, or foreign State.

Section 10. [1] No State shall enter into any Treaty, Alliance, or Confederation; grant Letters of Marque and Reprisal; coin Money; emit Bills of Credit; make any Thing but gold and silver Coin a Tender in Payment of Debts; pass any Bill of Attainder, ex post facto Law, or Law impairing the Obligation of Contracts, or grant any Title of Nobility.

[2] No State shall, without the Consent of the Congress, lay any Imposts or Duties on Imports or Exports, except what may be absolutely necessary for executing its inspection Laws: and the net Produce of all Duties and Imposts, laid by any State on Imports or Exports, shall be for the Use of the Treasury of the United States; and all such Laws shall be subject to the Revision and Controul of the Congress.

[3] No State shall, without the Consent of Congress, lay any duty of Tonnage, keep Troops, or Ships of War in time of Peace, enter into any Agreement or Compact with another State, or with a foreign Power, or engage in War, unless actually invaded, or in such imminent Danger as will not admit of delay.

Article II.

THE EXECUTIVE BRANCH

Section 1. [1] The executive Power shall be vested in a President of the United States of America. He shall hold his

Office during the Term of four Years, and, together with the Vice-President, chosen for the same Term, be elected, as follows.

[2] Each State shall appoint, in such Manner as the Legislature thereof may direct, a Number of Electors, equal to the whole Number of Senators and Representatives to which the State may be entitled in the Congress: but no Senator or Representative, or Person holding an Office of Trust or Profit under the United States, shall be appointed an Elector.

[3] [The Electors shall meet in their respective States, and vote by Ballot for two persons, of whom one at least shall not be an Inhabitant of the same State with themselves. And they shall make a List of all the Persons voted for, and of the Number of Votes for each; which List they shall sign and certify, and transmit sealed to the Seat of the Government of the United States, directed to the President of the Senate. The President of the Senate shall, in the Presence of the Senate and House of Representatives, open all the Certificates, and the Votes shall then be counted. The Person having the greatest Number of Votes shall be the President, if such Number be a Majority of the whole Number of Electors appointed; and if there be more than one who have such Majority, and have an equal Number of Votes, then the House of Representatives shall immediately chuse by Ballot one of them for President; and if no Person have a Majority, then from the five highest on the List the said House shall in like Manner chuse the President. But in chusing the President, the Votes shall be taken by States, the Representation from each State have one Vote; a quorum for this Purpose shall consist of a Member or Members from two thirds of the States, and a Majority of all the States

shall be necessary to a Choice. In every Case, after the Choice of the President, the Person having the greatest Number of Votes of the Electors shall be the Vice President. But if there should remain two or more who have equal Votes, the Senate shall chuse from them by Ballot the Vice-President.] (Note: Superseded by the Twelfth Amendment.)

[4] The Congress may determine the Time of chusing the Electors, and the Day on which they shall give their Votes; which Day shall be the same throughout the United States.

[5] No person except a natural born Citizen, or a Citizen of the United States, at the time of the Adoption of this Constitution, shall be eligible to the Office of President; neither shall any person be eligible to that Office who shall not have attained to the Age of thirty-five Years, and been fourteen Years a Resident within the United States.

[6] [In Case of the Removal of the President from Office, or of his Death, Resignation, or Inability to discharge the Powers and Duties of the said Office, the same shall devolve on the Vice President, and the Congress may by Law, provide for the Case of Removal, Death, Resignation or Inability, both of the President and Vice President, declaring what Officer shall then act as President, and such Officer shall act accordingly, until the Disability be removed, or a President shall be elected.] (Note: Changed by the Twenty-Fifth Amendment.)

[7] The President shall, at stated Times, receive for his Services, a Compensation, which shall neither be increased nor diminished during the Period for which he shall have been

elected, and he shall not receive within that Period any other Emolument from the United States, or any of them.

[8] Before he enter on the Execution of his Office, he shall take the following Oath or Affirmation: — "I do solemnly swear (or affirm) that I will faithfully execute the Office of President of the United States, and will to the best of my Ability, preserve, protect and defend the Constitution of the United States."

Section 2. [1] The President shall be Commander in Chief of the Army and Navy of the United States, and of the Militia of the several States, when called into the actual Service of the United States; he may require the Opinion in writing, of the principal Officer in each of the executive Departments, upon any subject relating to the Duties of their respective Offices, and he shall have Power to Grant Reprieves and Pardons for Offenses against the United States, except in Cases of Impeachment.

[2] He shall have Power, by and with the Advice and Consent of the Senate, to make Treaties, provided two-thirds of the Senators present concur; and he shall nominate, and by and with the Advice and Consent of the Senate, shall appoint Ambassadors, other public Ministers and Consuls, Judges of the supreme Court, and all other Officers of the United States, whose Appointments are not herein otherwise provided for, and which shall be established by Law: but the Congress may by Law vest the Appointment of such inferior Officers, as they think proper, in the President alone, in the Courts of Law, or in the Heads of Departments.

[3] The President shall have Power to fill up all Vacancies that may happen during the Recess of the Senate, by granting Commissions which shall expire at the End of their next Session.

Section 3. He shall from time to time give to the Congress Information of the State of the Union, and recommend to their Consideration such Measures as he shall judge necessary and expedient; he may, on extraordinary Occasions, convene both Houses, or either of them, and in Case of Disagreement between them, with Respect to the Time of Adjournment, he may adjourn them to such Time as he shall think proper; he shall receive Ambassadors and other public Ministers; he shall take Care that the Laws be faithfully executed, and shall Commission all the Officers of the United States.

Section 4. The President, Vice President and all civil Officers of the United States, shall be removed from Office on Impeachment for, and Conviction of, Treason, Bribery, or other high Crimes and Misdemeanors.

Article III.

THE JUDICIAL BRANCH

Section 1. The judicial Power of the United States, shall be vested in one supreme Court, and in such inferior Courts as the Congress may from time to time ordain and establish. The Judges, both of the supreme and inferior Courts, shall hold their Offices during good Behaviour, and shall, at stated Times, receive for their Services, a Compensation, which shall not be diminished during their Continuance in Office.

Section 2. [1] The judicial Power shall extend to all Cases, in Law and Equity, arising under this Constitution, the Laws of the United States, and Treaties made, or which shall be made, under their Authority; —to all Cases affecting Ambassadors, other public Ministers and Consuls; —to all Cases of admiralty and maritime Jurisdiction; —to Controversies to which the United States shall be a Party; —to Controversies between two or more States, —[between a State and Citizens of another State;—] (Note: Changed by the Eleventh Amendment.) between Citizens of different States; —between Citizens of the same State claiming Lands under Grants of different States, [and between a State, or the Citizens thereof, and foreign States, Citizens or Subjects.] (Note: Changed by the Eleventh Amendment.)

[2] In all Cases affecting Ambassadors, other public Ministers and Consuls, and those in which a State shall be Party, the supreme Court shall have original Jurisdiction. In all the other Cases before mentioned, the supreme Court shall have appellate Jurisdiction, both as to Law and Fact, with such Exceptions, and under such Regulations as the Congress shall make.

[3] The Trial of all Crimes, except in Cases of Impeachment, shall be by Jury; and such Trial shall be held in the State where the said Crimes shall have been committed; but when not committed within any State, the Trial shall be at such Place or Places as the Congress may by Law have directed.

Section 3. [1] Treason against the United States, shall consist only in levying War against them, or in adhering to their Enemies, giving them Aid and Comfort. No Person shall be convicted of Treason unless on the Testimony of two Witnesses to the same overt Act, or on Confession in open Court.

[2] The Congress shall have Power to declare the Punishment of Treason, but no Attainder of Treason shall work Corruption of Blood, or Forfeiture except during the Life of the Person attainted.

Article IV.

RELATION OF THE STATES TO EACH OTHER

Section 1. Full Faith and Credit shall be given in each State to the public Acts, Records, and judicial Proceedings of every other State; And the Congress may by general Laws prescribe the Manner in which such Acts, Records and Proceedings shall be proved, and the Effect thereof.

Section 2. [1] The Citizens of each State shall be entitled to all Privileges and Immunities of Citizens in the several States.

[2] A Person charged in any State with Treason, Felony, or other Crime, who shall flee from Justice, and be found in another State, shall on demand of the executive Authority of the State from which he fled, be delivered up, to be removed to the State having Jurisdiction of the Crime.

[3] [No Person held to Service or Labour in one State, under the Laws thereof, escaping into another, shall, in Consequence of

any Law or Regulation therein, be discharged from such Service or Labour, but shall be delivered up on Claim of the Party to whom such Service or Labour may be due.] (Note: Superseded by the Thirteenth Amendment.)

Section 3. [1] New States may be admitted by the Congress into this Union; but no new State shall be formed or erected within the Jurisdiction of any other State; nor any State be formed by the Junction of two or more States, or parts of States, without the Consent of the Legislatures of the States concerned as well as of the Congress.

[2] The Congress shall have Power to dispose of and make all needful Rules and Regulations respecting the Territory or other Property belonging to the United States; and nothing in this Constitution shall be so construed as to Prejudice any Claims of the United States, or of any particular State.

Section 4. The United States shall guarantee to every State in this Union a Republican Form of Government, and shall protect each of them against Invasion; and on Application of the Legislature, or of the Executive (when the Legislature cannot be convened) against domestic Violence.

Article V.

AMENDING THE CONSTITUTION

The Congress, whenever two thirds of both Houses shall deem it necessary, shall propose Amendments to this Constitution, or, on the Application of the Legislatures of two thirds of the several

States, shall call a Convention for proposing Amendments, which, in either Case, shall be valid to all Intents and Purposes, as Part of this Constitution, when ratified by the Legislatures of three fourths of the several States, or by Conventions in three fourths thereof, as the one or the other Mode of Ratification may be proposed by the Congress; Provided that no Amendment which may be made prior to the Year One thousand eight hundred and eight shall in any Manner affect the first and fourth Clauses in the Ninth Section of the first Article; and that no State, without its Consent, shall be deprived of its equal Suffrage in the Senate.

Article VI.

NATIONAL DEBTS

[1] All Debts contracted and Engagements entered into, before the Adoption of this Constitution, shall be as valid against the United States under this Constitution, as under the Confederation.

SUPREMACY OF THE NATIONAL GOVERNMENT

[2] This Constitution, and the Laws of the United States which shall be made in Pursuance thereof; and all Treaties made, or which shall be made, under the Authority of the United States, shall be the supreme Law of the Land; and the Judges in every State shall be bound thereby, any Thing in the Constitution or Laws of any State to the Contrary notwithstanding.

[3] The Senators and Representatives before mentioned, and the Members of the several State Legislatures, and all executive and judicial Officers, both of the United States and of the several States, shall be bound by Oath or Affirmation, to support this Constitution; but no religious Test shall ever be required as a Qualification to any Office or public Trust under the United States.

Article VII.

RATIFYING THE CONSTITUTION

The Ratification of the Conventions of nine States shall be sufficient for the Establishment of this Constitution between the States so ratifying the Same.

Done in Convention by the Unanimous Consent of the States present the Seventeenth Day of September in the Year of our Lord one thousand seven hundred and Eighty seven and of the Independence of the United States of America the Twelfth.

In Witness whereof We have hereunto subscribed our Names.

George Washington-President and deputy from Virginia

New Hampshire
John Langdon
Nicholas Gilman

Massachusetts
Nathaniel Gorham
Rufus King

Connecticut
Wm. Saml. Johnson
Roger Sherman

New York
Alexander Hamilton

New Jersey
Wil: Livingston
David Brearley
Wm. Paterson
Jona: Dayton

Pennsylvania
B Franklin
Thomas Mifflin
Robt Morris
Geo. Clymer
Thos. FitzSimons
Jared Ingersoll
James Wilson
Gouv Morris

Delaware
Geo: Read
Gunning Bedford jun
John Dickinson
Richard Basset
Jaco: Broom

Maryland
James McHenry
Dan of St Thos. Jenifer
Danl Carroll

Virginia
John Blair-
James Madison Jr.

North Carolina
Wm. Blount
Richd. Dobbs Spaight
Hu Williamson

South Carolina
J. Rutledge
Charles Cotesworth Pinckney
Charles Pinckney
Pierce Butler

Georgia
William Few
Abr Baldwin

Attest William Jackson Secretary

The Bill of Rights

Ratified, December 15, 1791

The First Amendment

Congress shall make no law respecting an establishment of religion, or prohibiting the free exercise thereof; or abridging the freedom of speech, or of the press, or the right of the people peaceably to assemble, and to petition the government for a redress of grievances.

The Second Amendment

A well-regulated militia, being necessary to the security of a free state, the right of the people to keep and bear arms, shall not be infringed.

The Third Amendment

No soldier shall, in time of peace be quartered in any house, without the consent of the owner, nor in time of war, but in a manner to be prescribed by law.

The Fourth Amendment

The right of the people to be secure in their persons, houses, papers, and effects, against unreasonable searches and seizures, shall not be violated, and no warrants shall issue, but upon probable cause, supported by oath or affirmation, and particularly describing the place to be searched, and the persons or things to be seized.

The Fifth Amendment

No person shall be held to answer for a capital, or otherwise infamous crime, unless on a presentment or indictment of a grand jury, except in cases arising in the land or naval forces, or in the militia, when in actual service in time of war or public danger; nor shall any person be subject for the same offense to be twice put in jeopardy of life or limb; nor shall be compelled in any criminal case to be a witness against himself, nor be deprived of life, liberty, or property, without due process of law; nor shall private property be taken for public use, without just compensation.

The Sixth Amendment

In all criminal prosecutions, the accused shall enjoy the right to a speedy and public trial, by an impartial jury of the state and district wherein the crime shall have been committed, which district shall have been previously ascertained by law, and to be informed of the nature and cause of the accusation; to be confronted with the witnesses against him; to have compulsory process for obtaining witnesses in his favor, and to have the assistance of counsel for his defense.

The Seventh Amendment

*In suits at common law, where the value in controversy
shall exceed twenty dollars, the right of trial by jury shall
be preserved, and no fact tried by a jury, shall be otherwise
reexamined in any court of the United States, than according to
the rules of the common law.*

The Eighth Amendment

*Excessive bail shall not be required, nor excessive fines imposed,
nor cruel and unusual punishments inflicted.*

The Ninth Amendment

*The enumeration in the Constitution, of certain rights, shall
not be construed to deny or disparage others retained by the
people.*

The Tenth Amendment

*The powers not delegated to the United States by the
Constitution, nor prohibited by it to the states, are reserved to
the states respectively, or to the people.*

SELECTED RECOMMENDED BOOKS	
Category	**Book (Notes)**
Classics/ Literature	Great Dialogues of Plato
	"Beowulf"—an Old English epic poem in the tradition of Germanic heroic legend
	Emma, Sense & Sensibility, Pride & Prejudice— books by Jane Austen
	Jane Eyre by Charlotte Bronte
	Tom Sawyer by Mark Twain
	Huckleberry Finn by Mark Twain
	Illiad—one of two major ancient Greek epic poems attributed to Homer
	Odessey—one of two major ancient Greek epic poems attributed to Homer
	Lord of the Rings by J.R.R. Tolkien
	The Hobbit by J.R.R. Tolkien
	Nineteen Eighty-four by George Orwell
	Animal Farm by George Orwell
	The Count of Monte Cristo by Alexandre Dumas
	Narnia series by C.S. Lewis
	King Arthur and His Knights by Thomas Malory
	Shakespearean Sonnets by Shakespeare
	The Scarlet Pimpernel by Emmuska Orczy
	The Strange Case of Dr. Jekyll and Mr. Hyde by Robert Louis Stevenson
	To Kill a Mockingbird by Harper Lee
	Uncle Tom's Cabin by Harriet Beecher Stowe

| SELECTED RECOMMENDED BOOKS ||
Category	Book (Notes)
History	1776 by David McCullough
	The Radicalism of the American Revolution by Gordon S. Wood
	The Rise and Fall of the Third Reich by William Shirer
	When a Nation Forgets God by Erwin Lutzer
	The History of the World series OR The Story of the World by Susan Wise Bauer
	A History of the American People by Paul Johnson
	The Indestructible Book: The Story of the Bible and the Sacrifices of its English Translators by Ken Connolly
	One Life to Give: Martyrdom and the Making of the American Revolution by John Fanestil
	The Indispensables: The Diverse Soldier-Mariners Who Shaped the Country, Formed the Navy, and Rowed Washington Across the Delaware by Patrick K. O'Donnell
	The Seven Military Classics of Ancient China (History and Warfare) by Ralph D. Sawyer
Warnings	Battle for the American Mind: Uprooting a Century of Miseducation Hardcover by Pete Hegsweth and David Goodwin
	The Coddling of the American Mind: How Good Intentions and Bad Ideas Are Setting Up a Generation for Failure by Greg Lukianoff and Jonathan Haidt
	The Great Reset (A Warning) by Alex Jones

SELECTED RECOMMENDED BOOKS	
Category	**Book (Notes)**
Warnings	The Dying Citizen by Dr. Victor Davis Hanson
(Continued)	The Road to Serfdom by Friedrich Hayek
Political/	Various Publications by Dr. Steve Turley
Current	The Clash of Civilizations and the
Events	Remaking of World Order by Samuel P.
	Huntington
	Fault Lines by Voddie Baucham
	Culture Wars by James Davison Hunter
	American Injustice by Jon Paul Mac Issac
	The Psychology of Totalitarianism by Mattias Desmet
	Inside American Education by Thomas Sowell
	How to Destroy America in Three Easy Steps by Ben Shapiro
Morals/	Holy Bible
Religion/	Book of Mormon
Faith	Talmud
	Torah
	Works written by C.S. Lewis
	Saved From What? by R.C. Sproul
	The Parables of Jesus by R.C. Sproul (pretty much any or all R.C. Sproul books)
	You Are What You Love by James Smith
Biographies	Nimitz by E.B. Potter
	The Life and Times of Frederick Douglas (African American) by Frederick Douglass

SELECTED RECOMMENDED BOOKS	
Category	**Book (Notes)**
Biographies (Continued)	Life of Washington by Anna Reed
	Waterman: The Life and Times of Duke Kahanamoku by David Davis
	Samuel Adams: The Life of an American Revolutionary by John K. Alexander
Leadership	Leadership Lessons of the Navy SEALS: Battle-Tested Strategies for Creating Successful Organizations and Inspiring Extraordinary Results by Jeff Cannon and Jon Cannon
	Extreme Ownership: How U.S. Navy SEALs Lead and Win by Jocko Willink
	You're a Leader, Now What by Mick Spiers
	The Leader's Bookshelf (and the recommended books therein) by ADM James G Stavridis USN (Ret) and R. Manning Ancell
	The Art of War by Sun-Tzu (Author) by Ralph D. Sawyer
Wealth/ Economics	Think and Grow Rich by Napoleon Hill
	Thou Shall Prosper by Rabbi Daniel Lapin
	Economic Facts and Fallacies by Thomas Sowell
	Discrimination and Disparities by Thomas Sowell
LIBRARY ONLY **(Do not purchase)**	Rules for Radicals by Saul Alinski
	Values by Mark Carney
	The Great Reset by Klaus Schwab
	Hegemony How-To: A Roadmap for Radicals by Jonathan Smucker

Author Bio

Originally from historic Connecticut, Kyle A. Stone grew up steeped in America's history and learning of its heroes. A man of faith and a student of history, politics, leadership, and global events, he keenly observes trends that impact the citizens of the United States.

In his civilian career, Kyle is a Technical Program Manager for a popular financial technology company and has worked as a software engineer and development manager for known global organizations. In his military profession, Kyle is a veteran in the U.S. Coast Guard Reserve, having served in Coast Guard "blue" and Department of Defense "green" uniforms domestically and overseas.

Kyle holds a Master of Arts in Defense and Strategic Studies from the United States Naval War College, a Master in Business Administration from the University of Washington, a Bachelor of Arts in History (minor in Psychology) from Brigham Young University, and an Associate in Information Technology from The Institutes. He also holds multiple professional and technical certifications, including the Project Management Professional (PMP) designation.

When not balancing multiple responsibilities, he can usually be found exercising, hiking, reading, or writing. He lives a quiet existence in the west.

References

1894. *Publications of the American Jewish Historical Society: Volume 2*. American Jewish Historical Society. https://doi.org/https://play.google.com/books/reader?id=H6UyAQAAMAAJ&pg=GBS.PP14&hl=en.

"1993 U.S. Apology Resolution." 2022. Hawaiian Kingdom - 1993 U.S. Apology Resolution. Hawaiian Kingdom. (October). https://www.hawaiiankingdom.org/apology.shtml.

Adams, Abigail. 1776. "Abigail Adams to John Adams, 31 March 1776." *Founders Online*. National Archives. https://founders.archives.gov/documents/ Adams/04-01-02-0241. [Original source: The Adams Papers, Adams Family Correspondence, vol. 1, December 1761–May 1776, ed. Lyman H. Butterfield. Cambridge, MA: Harvard University Press, 1963, pp. 369–371.].

Adams, Abigail. 1797. "Abigail Adams to John Adams, 13 February 1797." *Founders Online*. National Archives. https://founders.archives.gov/documents/ Adams/04-11-02-0293. [Original source: The Adams Papers, Adams Family Correspondence, vol. 11, July 1795–February 1797, ed. Margaret A. Hogan, C. James Taylor, Sara Martin, Neal E. Millikan, Hobson Woodward, Sara B. Sikes, and Gregg L. Lint.

Cambridge, MA: Harvard University Press, 2013, pp. 560–562.].

Adams, John. 1780. "John Adams to Abigail Adams, 12 May 1780." *Founders Online*. National Archives. https:// founders.archives.gov/documents/Adams/04-03-02- 0258. [Original source: The Adams Papers, Adams Family Correspondence, vol. 3, April 1778–September 1780, ed. L. H. Butterfield and Marc Friedlaender. Cambridge, MA: Harvard University Press, 1973, pp. 341–343.].

Adams, John. 1781. "John Adams to John Quincy Adams, 18 May 1781." *Founders Online*. National Archives. https://founders.archives.gov/documents/ Adams/04- 04-02-0082. [Original source: The Adams Papers, Adams Family Correspondence, vol. 4, October 1780–September 1782, ed. L.H Butterfield and Marc Friedlaender. Cambridge, MA: Harvard University Press, 1973, pp. 117–118.].

Adams, Samuel. 1884. *A Book of New England Legends and Folk Lore in Prose and Poetry*. Boston: Roberts Brothers. https://play.google.com/books/ reader?id=wMsrAAAAYAAJ&pg=GBS.PR2&hl=en.

Adams, Samuel. 1908. *The Writings of Samuel Adams v. IV.* Edited by Cushing, Harry A. New York: G.P. Putnam's Sons. https://doi.org/https://archive.org/ details/ cu31924092891195/page/n7/mode/2up.

Allgor, Catherine. 2007. *A Perfect Union: Dolley Madison and the Creation of the American Nation.* New York: Henry Holt and Company. https://books. google.com/books?id=Vz9QGFbiVqsC&pg=PA85&lpg=PA85&dq=%22This+will+be+the+cause+of+war%22+Dolley&source=bl&ots=q_LXuHCXDf&sig=ACfU3U3j4IM2fqaoEAQwT OWs-xaGE3rBLg&hl=en&sa=X&ved=2ahUK EwiJ0sus_oH7AhXQMzQIHdmNBmIQ6AF-6BAgkEAM#v=onepage&q=%22This%20will%20 be%20the%20cause%20of%20war%22%20 Dolley&f=false.

"Boise Strikes Gold." 2022. *Totally Boise.* (October). https:// totallyboise.com/History.

Bradford, William. 1898. *Of Plimouth Plantation.* Boston; Project Gutenberg, 2022. https://www.gutenberg. org/ files/24950/24950-h/24950-h.htm.

"Brief Biography of Thomas Jefferson." 2022. (web page). *Thomas Jefferson's Monticello.* Thomas Jefferson Foundation. https://www.monticello.org/ thomas-jefferson/brief-biography-of-jefferson/.

"Creating the United States: Creating the Declaration of Independence." 2022. *Library of Congress.* https:// www. loc.gov/exhibits/creating-the-united-states/ interactives/ declaration-of-independence/equal/ index.html.

Davis, David. 2015. *Waterman: The Life and Times of Duke Kahanamoku.* Lincoln: University of Nebraska Press.

Davis, Shelby C. 2022. "Our Sacred Honor." Diana Davis Spencer Foundation. https://ddsfoundation.org/our-sacred-honor/.

"Debt." 2022. (webpage). *Thomas Jefferson's Monticello.* Thomas Jefferson Foundation. https://www.monticello.org/research-education/thomas-jefferson-encyclopedia/debt/.

"Delegates to the Constitutional Convention." 2020. (web page). *This Nation.* (January). https://www.thisnation.com/government/delegates-to-the-constitutional-convention/.

"Emma Edwards Green Papers." 2022. *Idaho State Archives.* Idaho State Historical Society. (October). https://idahohistory.contentdm.oclc.org/digital/collection/p16281coll37/id/288/rec/1.

Fanestil, John. 2021. "Nathan Hale: The Inside Story of an American Revolutionary." *John Fanestil: Life & Death, Past & Present, Here & There.* (October). https:// www.johnfanestil.com/post/nathan-hale-the-inside-story-of-an-american-revolutionary. [Original Source: Watson, Ebenezer. 1775. *Watson's Register, and Connecticut Almanack, for the Year of Our Lord, 1776.* Hartford, CT: Ebenezer Watson. 8, 24].

"Fewer Years of Healthy Life for Native Hawaiians, UH Study Finds." 2019. *University of Hawai'I News.* (November). https://www.hawaii.edu/news/2019/11/05/hawaii-hale-study/.

Fox, Frank W. and LeGrand L. Baker. 1976. "Wise Men Raised Up." *The Church of Jesus Christ of Latter-Day Saints.* https://www.churchofjesuschrist.org/study/ensign/1976/06/wise-men-raised-up?lang=eng.

Franklin, Benjamin. 1766. "Arator. On the Price of Corn, and the Management of the Poor 29 November 1766." *Founders Online.* National Archives. https://founders.archives.gov/documents/Franklin/01-13-02-0194. [Original source: The Papers of Benjamin Franklin, vol. 13, January 1 through December 31, 1766, ed. Leonard W. Labaree. New Haven and London: Yale University Press, 1969, pp. 510–516.]

"Giving Thanks Can Make You Happier." 2021. (web page). *Harvard Health Publishing.* Harvard Medical School. (August). https://www.health.harvard.edu/healthbeat/giving-thanks-can-make-you-happier.

Gosling, Tony. 2018. "1637 Pequot Massacre: The Real Story of the Annual U.S. Thanksgiving." *The Land Is Ours.* https://doi.org/https://tlio.org.uk/1637-pequotmassacre-%e2%80%8bthe real-story-of-thanksgiving/#comments.

Green, Emma Edwards. 2022. "Description of the Idaho State Seal." *Idaho: Official Government Website.* https://gov.idaho.gov/idaho-state-seal/.

Hanson, Victor Davis. 2021. *The Dying Citizen: How Progressive Elites, Tribalism, and Globalization Are Destroying the Idea of America.* New York: Basic Books.

Hegseth, Pete, and David Goodwin. 2022. *Battle for the American Mind: Uprooting a Century of Miseducation.* Read by Pete Hegseth and David Goodwin. Audible audio ed. 9 hr., 23 min.

Holmquist, Annie. 2018. "Aleksandr Solzhenitsyn's Forgotten Lesson on Good and Evil: Annie Holmquist." *FEE Stories.* Foundation for Economic Education. (November). https://fee.org/articles/aleksandr-solzhenitsyns-forgotten-lesson-on-good-and-evil/.

Hutchinson, E.J. 2018. "Can the Liberal Arts Save Our Souls?" *The Imaginative Conservative.* (July). https://theimaginativeconservative.org/2018/07/liberal- arts-save-soul-e-j-hutchinson.html.

Jefferson, Thomas. 1789. "From Thomas Jefferson to Joseph Willard, 24 March 1789." *Founders Online.* National Archives. https://founders.archives.gov/documents/Jefferson/01-14-02-0437. [Original source: The Papers of Thomas Jefferson, vol. 14, 8 October 1788–26 March 1789, ed. Julian P. Boyd. Princeton: Princeton University Press, 1958, pp. 697–699.].

Jefferson, Thomas. 1801. "III. First Inaugural Address 04 March 1801." *Founders Online*. National Archives. https://founders.archives.gov/documents/Jefferson/01-33-02-0116-0004 [Original source: *National Intelligencer,* 4 March 1801].

Jefferson, Thomas. 1815. "Thomas Jefferson to John Adams, 10 June 1815." *Founders Online*. National Archives. https://founders.archives.gov/documents/Jefferson/03-08-02-0425. [Original source: The Papers of Thomas Jefferson, Retirement Series, vol. 8, 1 October 1814 to 31 August 1815, ed. J. Jefferson Looney. Princeton: Princeton University Press, 2011, pp. 522–523.].

Jefferson, Thomas. 1816. "Thomas Jefferson to Pierre Samuel Du Pont de Nemours, 24 April 1816." *Founders Online*. National Archives. https://founders.archives.gov/documents/Jefferson/03-09-02-0471. [Original source: The Papers of Thomas Jefferson, Retirement Series, vol. 9, September 1815 to April 1816, ed. J. Jefferson Looney. Princeton: Princeton University Press, 2012, pp. 699–702.].

Jefferson, Thomas. 1998. Notes on the State of Virginia. Penguin Classics S. Harlow, England: Penguin Books.

Jefferson, Thomas. 2012. "The Declaration of Independence." In *The Constitution of the United States of America and Selected Writings of the Founding Fathers.* New York: Barnes & Noble.

Jefferson, Thomas. 2022. (web page). *Thomas Jefferson's Monticello.* Thomas Jefferson Foundation. https://www.monticello.org/thomas-jefferson/jefferson-s-three-greatest-achievements/the-declaration/transcript-of-the-rough-of-the-declaration/.

Jewell, William. 2011. *The Golden Cabinet of True Treasure.* London: John Crosley, 1612; Ann Arbor: Text Creation Partnership. http://name.umdl.umich.edu/A04486.0001.001.

Kaufman, Yosef. 2022. "Haym Salomon: The Man Who Financed the American Revolution." *Chabad.org.* https://www.chabad.org/library/article_cdo/aid/5175340/jewish/Haym-Salomon-The-Man-Who-Financed-the-American-Revolution.htm.

Klos, Stan. 2013. "Dolley Payne Madison." *Dolley Madison.* https://www.dolleymadison.org/2013/07/dolley-madison.html.

Lincoln, Abraham. 2018. "Lyceum Address." *Abraham Lincoln Online.* https://www.abrahamlincolnonline.org/lincoln/speeches/lyceum.htm [Original source: *The Collected Works of Abraham Lincoln.* 1953. Ed. Roy P. Basler].

Lockwood, George B. 1905. *The New Harmony Movement.* New York: D. Appleton and Company. Google Books, 2022.

Madison, James. 1788. "*The Federalist* Number 47, [30 January] 1788." *Founders Online.* National Archives. https://founders.archives.gov/documents/ Madison/01-10-02-0266. [Original source: The Papers of James Madison, vol. 10, 27 May 1787–3 March 1788, ed. Robert A. Rutland, Charles F. Hobson, William M. E. Rachal, and Frederika J. Teute. Chicago: The University of Chicago Press, 1977, pp. 448–454.].

Madison, James. 1792. "*Property.* Papers 14:266—68, [29 March] 1792." The Founders' Constitution Volume 1, Chapter 16, Document 23. https://press-pubs. uchicago.edu/founders/documents/v1ch16s23.html. [Original source: The Papers of James Madison. Edited by William T. Hutchinson et al. Chicago and London: University of Chicago Press, 1962—77 (vols. 1—10); Charlottesville: University Press of Virginia, 1977-- (vols. 11--).].

Malcolm, John. 2021. "Are Parents Being Tagged as 'Domestic Terrorists' by the FBI? Justice Department Needs to Show Its Cards." *The Heritage Foundation.* https:// www.heritage.org/crime-and-justice/ commentary/ are-parents-being-tagged-domestic-terrorists-the-fbi-justice.

Marcin, Tim. 2016. "Fidel Castro's Amasses a Massive Fortune in Communist Cuba." *Yahoo News.* (28 November). https://news.yahoo.com/fidel-castros-amassed-massive-fortune-142104351.html.

Mathews, M.B. 2022. (web page). "The Party of Violence." *American Thinker.* (July). https://www.american-thinker.com/articles/2022/07/the_party_of_violence.html.

Military Benefits. 2020. "Top Reasons Gen Z Should Join the Military." *Military Benefits.* Veteran.com. (March). https://veteran.com/reasons-gen-z-military/.

Miller, Julie. 2022. "A Republic If You Can Keep It: Elizabeth Willing Powel, Benjamin Franklin, and the James McHenry Journal." *Library of Congress.* (January). https://blogs.loc.gov/manuscripts/2022/01/a-republic-if-you-can-keep-it-elizabeth-willing-powel-benjamin-franklin-and-the-james-mchenry-journal/.

Monroe, James. 1818. *A Narrative of a Tour of Observation Made During the Summer of 1817.* Phildelphia: S.A. Mitchell and H. Ames. https://play.google.com/books/reader?id=srZEAAAAIAAJ&pg=GBS.PA2&printsec=frontcover.

Morris, Robert. 1973. *The Papers of Robert Morris, 1781-1784. v.1.* Pittsburgh: University of Pittsburgh Press. https://doi.org/https://digital.library.pitt.edu/islandora/object/pitt%3A31735060481813/viewer#page/120/mode/2up.

Morse, Jedidiah. D.D. 1824. *Annals of the American Revolution.* Hartford: Oliver D Cook & Sons. https://play.google.com/books/reader?id=Tbqu-JQo5Ic0C&pg=GBS.PP8&hl=en.

Mount, Steve. 5 October 2022. "Speech of Benjamin Franklin" (web page). *U.S. Constitution.* https://www.usconstitution.net/franklin.html. [Original Source: *The Debate on the Constitution Part 1: September 1787 to February 1788.* Bernard Bailyn. Copyright 1990 Published at Library of Congress. 3-6.]

Mussomeli, Joseph. 2020. "The Human Longing for Gratitude: A Thanksgiving Reflection." *The Imaginative Conservative.* (November). https://theimaginativeconservative.org/2020/11/ human-longing-gratitude-thanksgiving-reflection-timeless-joseph-mussomeli.html.

Online Etymology Dictionary. 2022. https://www.etymonline. com/search?q=charity.

Ortner, Mary J. 2001. "Captain Nathan Hale (1755 – 1776)." *Connecticut Sons of the American Revolution.* https://www.sarconnecticut.org/captain-nathan-hale-1755-1776-2/.

Orwell, George. 1945. *Animal Farm.* Adelaide: The University of Adelaide Library. https://www.openrightslibrary. com/animal-farm-ebook/.

Orwell, George. 1949. *Nineteen Eighty-Four.* New York: Harcourt Brace Jovanovich, Inc.

Paine, Thomas. 2012. "The American Crisis: Crisis no.1." In *The Constitution of the United States of America and*

Selected Writings of the Founding Fathers. New York: Barnes & Noble.

Peters, Madison C. 1911. *Haym Salomon: The Financier of the Revolution, An Unwritten Chapter in American History*. New York: The Trow Press. https://doi.org/ https://books.google.com/books?id=zrULAAAA-IAAJ&printsec=frontcover&source=gbs_ge_summary_r&cad=0#v=onepage&q&f=false.

Peterson, Jordan B. 2018. *12 Rules for Life: An Antidote to Chaos*. Canada: Random House.

Philo, L. Curtius, L. Hostilia Scaura, and P. Iunius Brutus. 2019. "Roman Virtues." *Roman Republic Respublica Roman*. https://romanrepublic.org/roma/ bibliotheca/ roman-virtues/.

Plato. 1959. *Great Dialogues of Plato*. Translated by W.H.D. Rouse. New York: Signet Classics; Internet Archive EBook, 2022. https://archive.org/details/greatdialoguesof00plat_0.

Pokorski, Robin. 2022. "George Washington's Library." *George Washington's Mount Vernon*. Mount Vernon Ladies' Association. (October). https://www.mountvernon.org/library/digitalhistory/digital-encyclopedia/ article/george-washingtons-library/.

Pratt, Orson, Smith, Joseph., and Coutant, Charles. 1830. *The Book of Mormon: Another Testament of Jesus Christ*.

Salt Lake: The Church of Jesus Christ of Latter-Day Saints.

"Professor: Children Belong to the State, Not Parents." 2013. *The College Fix.* https://www.thecollegefix.com/professor-children-belong-to-the-state-not-parents-video/.

Rafael. 2022. "Cuba's Monthly Salaries: How They Compare to the U.S." *Auténtica Cuba.* (September). https:// autenticacuba.com/ cubas-monthly-salaries-how-they-compare-to-the-us/.

Rowlandson, Mary. 1682. *Captivity and Restoration.* Boston; Project Gutenberg, 2009. https://www.gutenberg. org/ files/851/851-h/851-h.htm.

Rush, Benjamin. 1811. "To John Adams from Benjamin Rush, 20 July 1811." *Founders Online.* National Archives. https://founders.archives.gov/documents/Adams/99-02-02-5659. [This is an Early Access document from The Adams Papers. It is not an authoritative final version.].

"Sale of Books to the Library of Congress (1815)." 2022. (web page). *Thomas Jefferson's Monticello.* Thomas Jefferson Foundation. https://www.monticello.org/research-education/thomas-jefferson-encyclopedia/sale-books-library-congress-1815/.

Scallan, Ben. 2022. "World Economic Forum Worried Public Less Trusting of 'Elites.'" *Gript.* https://gript. ie/

world-economic-forum-worried-public-less-trusting-of-
elites/.

Schoolfield, John. 1976. "Drum Beat:Tales of
the Revolution." *Ludington Daily News.*
https://doi.org/https://books. google.com/
books?id=9pNaAAAAIBAJ&printsec=-
frontcover&source=gbs_all_issues_r&cad=1#v=one-
page&q&f=true.

"The People Assume We Are Just Going Back to the Good
Old World Which We Had-Klaus Schwab (2020)."
Woke Media. May 2, 2021. Video, 0:01:09, https://
www.youtube.com/watch?v=x-9ZppjeQQo.

"Australian eSafety commissioner Julie Inman Grant speaks
about "recalibration" of freedom of speech." Klausica
Schwabescu. May 3, 2022. Video, 0:00:26, https://
www.youtube.com/watch?v=ydW6wDMQHX8.

"Bishop Sheen Prophecy 50 Years Ago." Catholic Chroma
Channel. November 20, 2020. Video, 0:24:32, https://
www.youtube.com/ watch?v=kOKlHUqOsIM&t=1s.

Siller, Stephen. 2022. "Never Forget." *Tunnel to Towers
Foundation.*   https://t2t.org/Stephen's Story.

Siller, Frank. 2022. "Never Forget." *Tunnel to Towers
Foundation.*   https://t2t.org/9-11-never-forget/
frank-siller/.

Straub, Steve. 2012. "Noah Webster-'History of the United
States', Chapter XIX (Advice No. 49 in His 'Advice

to the Young'); 1832." *The Federalist Papers.* https://
thefederalistpapers.org/founders/noah-webster/ noah-
webster-history-of-the-united-states-chapter-xix-advice-
no-49-in-his-advice-to-the-young-1832.

"Thanksgiving Proclamation of 1789." 2022. (web page).
George Washington's Mount Vernon. Mount Vernon
Ladies' Association. (September). https://www.
mountvernon.org/education/primary-sources-2/ article/
thanksgiving-proclamation-of-1789/.

"The Best Way to Learn Critical Thinking." Bite-Sized
Philosophy. December 7, 2017. Video, 0:04:01, https://
www.youtube.com/watch?v=x0vUsxhMczI.

"Thomas Jefferson: Jefferson's Library." 2022. (web page).
Library of Congress. https://www.loc.gov/exhibits/
jefferson/jefflib.html.

Thomas, Robert K., & Shirley Wilkes Thomas. 1976.
"Declaration of Dependence: Teaching Patriotism in
the Home." *The Church of Jesus Christ of Latter-Day
Saints.* https://www.churchofjesuschrist.org/study/
ensign/1976/06/declaration-of-dependence-teaching-
patriotism-in-the-home?lang=eng.

"Traditions." 2022. (web page). *Dickinson College.*
https://www.dickinson.edu/info/20048/
history_of_the_college/1031/traditions.

Turley, Steve PhD, interview by Kyle A. Stone. 2022.
Virtues (August 1).

"World Economic Forum Presents: The Great Reset—
"You'll own nothing, and you'll be happy."." Darrell
Vermilion. November 14, 2020. Video, 0:01:32,
https://www.youtube.com/watch?v=4zUjsEaKbkM.

Washington, George. 1776. "From George Washington
to Samuel Washington, 18 December 1776." *Founders
Online*. National Archives. https://founders.archives.
gov/documents/Washington/03-07-02-0299.
[Original source: The Papers of George Washington.
Revolutionary War Series. Vol. 7. 21 October 1776–5
January 1777. Ed. Philander D. Chase. Charlottesville:
University Press of Virginia. 1997. 369–372.].

Washington, George. 1781. "From George Washington
to Robert Morris, 17 August 1781," *Founders Online*.
National Archives. https://founders.archives.gov/
documents/Washington/99-01-02-06710). (Temporary
Link per the National Archives)

Washington, George. 1794. "From George Washington to
Charles Mynn Thruston, 10 August 1794." *Founders
Online*. National Archives. https://founders.archives.
gov/documents/Washington/05-16-02-0376. [Original
source: The Papers of George Washington, Presidential
Series, vol. 16, 1 May–30 September 1794, ed. David
R. Hoth and Carol S. Ebel. Charlottesville: University
of Virginia Press, 2011, pp. 547–548.].

Washington, George. 1799. "George Washington's Last Will
and Testament, 9 July 1799." *Founders Online*. National

Archives. https://founders.archives.gov/ documents/ Washington/06-04-02-0404-0001. [Original source: The Papers of George Washington, Retirement Series, vol. 4, 20 April 1799–13 December 1799, ed. W. W. Abbot. Charlottesville: University Press of Virginia, 1999, pp. 479–511.].

Williams, Clayton. 1836. *Come, Come Ye Saints.* Salt Lake: The Church of Jesus Christ of Latter-Day Saints 2023. https://www.churchofjesuschrist.org/music/text/hymns/ come-come-ye-saints?lang=eng

Wilson, Gaye, Pierce, Dianne, and Kristi Robinson. 2022. "The Merry Affair." *Thomas Jefferson's Monticello.* Thomas Jefferson Foundation. https://www.monticello. org/ exhibits-events/livestreams-videos-and-podcasts/ merry-affair-ichepod/.

Wolf, Edwin, and Kevin J. Hayes. 2006. *The Library of Benjamin Franklin.* Philadelphia; Google Books: 2022. https://books.google.com/ books?id=ibgiSlbMDPUC&printsec.

URGENT PLEA!

Thank you for reading my book!

I really appreciate all of your feedback, and I love hearing what you have to say.

I need your input to make the next version of this book and my future books better.

Please take two minutes now to leave a helpful review on Amazon letting me know what you thought of the book:

ValuesWeHoldDear.com

Thanks so much!
Kyle A. Stone

.

Made in the USA
Monee, IL
04 April 2025

15169180R00133